Wilmington

David Heuring

Then and Now

Conrad Lowman

By Andrew Koeppel

Foreword by Anne Russell

Photographic Contributor: Conrad Lowman

Published By: Andrew Koeppel
P.O. Box 4443
Wilmington, NC 28406

Printed in Wilmington, North Carolina

Library of Congress Catalogue Number: Applied For

The abbreviations below indicate the names beside them.
LCFHS - Lower Cape Fear Historical Society
NHCPL - New Hanover County Public Library

Foreword

When Andrew Koeppel chose to make his home in Wilmington, he brought us a new vantage point. Wilmington Then and Now is Andy's effort to put the contemporary city into context with its history. The old and new photographs in the book depict what used to be in comparison with what currently exists. Old timers may see the many changes which alter our landscape, and newcomers may better understand the ambience of yesterday.

The wonderful thing about history is that it belongs to all of us. Each historian's perspective builds on the work of other historians, providing us with a comprehensive view. Wilmington Then and Now fills a niche, and I am grateful to Andy for his dedication to making his own vision become a published reality.

Anne Russell
Author of **Wilmington a Pictorial History**

Acknowledgements

There are undoubtedly many parallels between making a movie, manufacturing a product and publishing a book. Each of these endeavors requires the participation of a team of dedicated individuals. Although one person is usually needed to coordinate the enterprise, he would be unable to complete the undertaking without the contributions of others.

Three people deserve particular praise for their efforts. Robert Little of The Wilmington Printing Company provided the guidance needed to publish a book at a high standard of quality. Second, Conrad Lowman achieved a level of photographic excellence worthy of the praise of other members of his profession. Third, Anne Russell encouraged the publication of this book from its inception. She also provided valuable perspectives based upon her knowledge of the Cape Fear Region.

A special commendation must be given to my wife, Eileen. She was tolerant of the time needed for this project and was a positive influence whenever difficulties arose.

In addition the people listed below were exceptionally helpful. Although they offered differing types of assistance, none of them would object to being listed with the others.

John Allen	Todd Hamm	Christine Perez
Regis John Alexoudis	Bobby Harrelson	Jim Pleasants
Richard Andrews	Susan Harrington	John Pistolis
Wes Beckner	Mary Hatcher	Whitey Prevatte
Rush Beeler	Robert Henry	Bill Raney
Susan Taylor Block	David Heuring	Henry Rehder
Tim Bottoms	John Hicks	Henry Rehder, Jr.
Betty Bowden	Sam Hill	Charlie Rivenbark
Nancy Bridgers	Beverly Ingram	Peggy Roberts
Bob Bryant	Toni Isbell	Jon Rosborough
Don Brown	Steve Jacobs	Gena Berta Roundtree
Dan Cameron	Virginia Jennewein	Suzanne Nash Ruffin
Frank Conlon	Mary Ann Jones	Milton Schaeffer
Merle Chamberlain	Billy King	Joe Sheppard
Don Clements	Tommy King	Penny Spicer Sidbury
Derrell Clerk	Tricia King	Bill Smith
Chick Coleman	Michael Kingoff	Mark Stinneford
Bill Creasy	William Kingoff	Bill Stokes
Dick Daughtry	Henry Longley	Billy Sutton
Barbara Downing	Gloria Ludwig	Beverly Tetterton
Jeff DuBose	Bill McEachern	Jerry Todd
Marion DuBose	George McEachern	Harry Tuchmayer
Mark Edwards	Tabitha Hutaff McEachern	Ed Turberg
Pamela O'Brien Eldridge	Pete McKenzie	Ray Twaro
John Elliot	Dan Marett	Joyce Vietto
Janine Ferrell	Sherry Mason	Harry Warren
Maxine Fishero	Matt Mathews	Calvin Wells
Karen Fox	Perry Maxwell	Rick Willetts
Bill Gage	Bob Murphrey	Kent Williams
Thomas Haddon	Jim Murrill	Charlie Wilson
Tommy Hagood	Dave Paynter	Allan Zimmer

Introduction

The purpose of this book is to illustrate locations and buildings and to indicate how they have changed. During the last forty years, Wilmington has experienced a significant transformation. When the Atlantic Coast Line Railroad moved its headquarters to Florida, the city began a new era both economically and structurally.

Wilmington Then and Now gives people who remember the Cape Fear Region before 1960 an opportunity to relive memories of their younger days. It also allows those individuals to witness the way in which the area appeared to previous generations.

Although many people relocated or returned to Wilmington during the 1970's and the 80's, with the completion of Interstate 40, the rate of increase in population and economic development surpassed the numbers that had been anticipated. The region became the home to a great many new residents, including the writer, who wanted a contemporary book to help them learn about Wilmington's past.

It is one thing to hear someone say that a certain structure was located on a corner where a recently constructed building is today. To actually see two pictures of that location illustrating the past and the present is much more meaningful.

As described in the table of contents, Wilmington Then and Now begins with geographic locations downtown. A series of chapters follow that highlight important aspects of daily life. Although some of the "now" portions may become "then" in a few years, subsequent printings can continually show us how Wilmington will evolve in the future.

Andrew Koeppel
August, 2000

TABLE OF CONTENTS

Table of contents for maps:

CHAPTER 1

MAPS

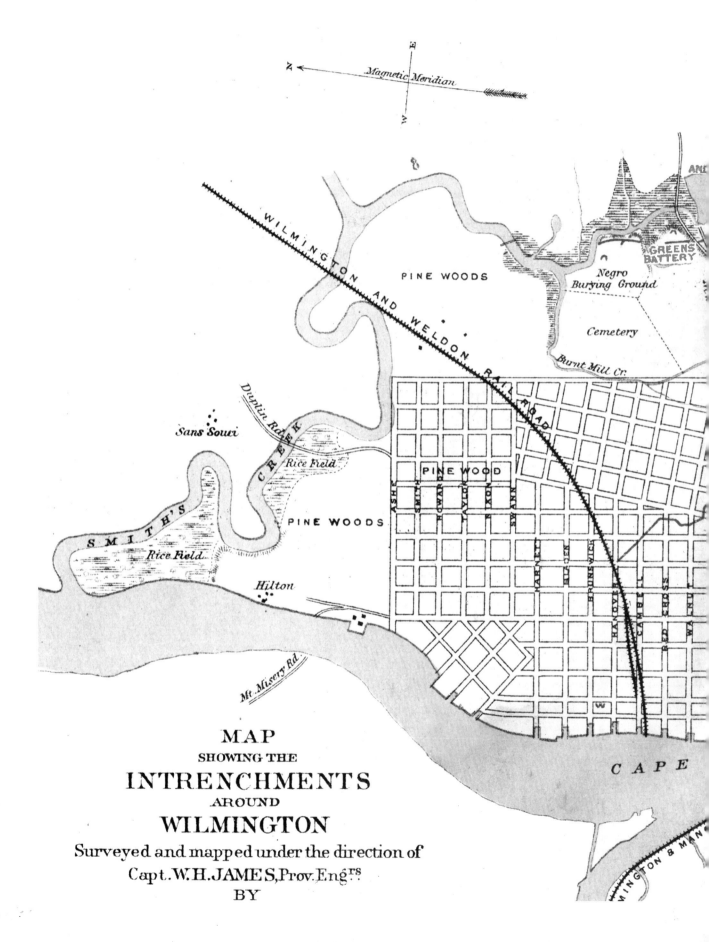

MAP
SHOWING THE
INTRENCHMENTS
AROUND
WILMINGTON
Surveyed and mapped under the direction of
Capt. W.H. JAMES, Prov. Eng.rs
BY

WILMINGTON 1929

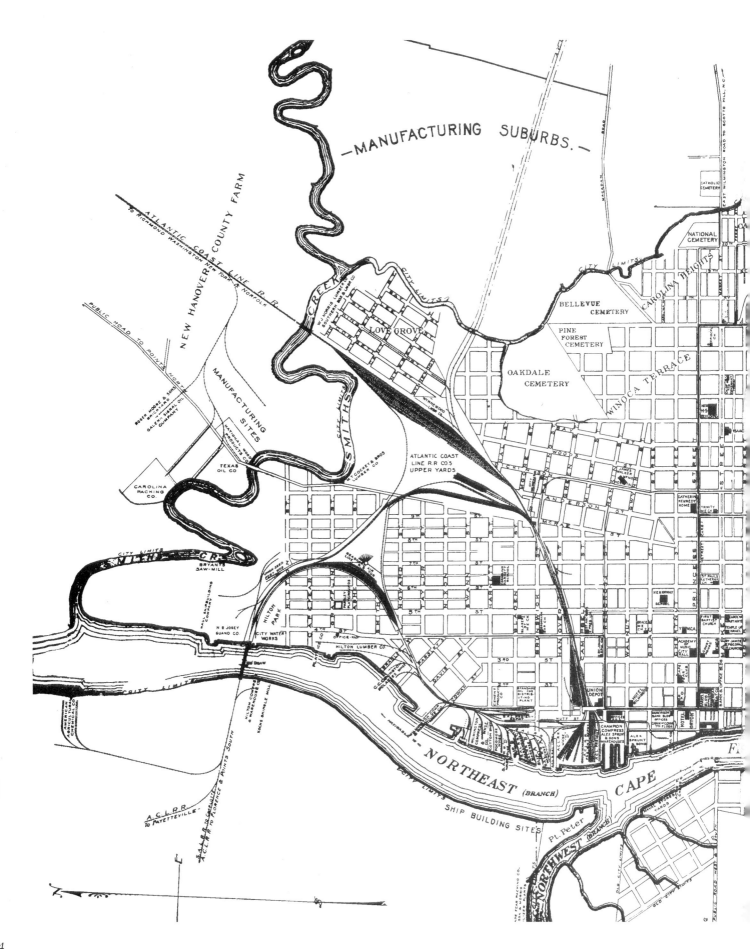

MANUFACTURING SUBURBS.

4

WILMINGTON 1863

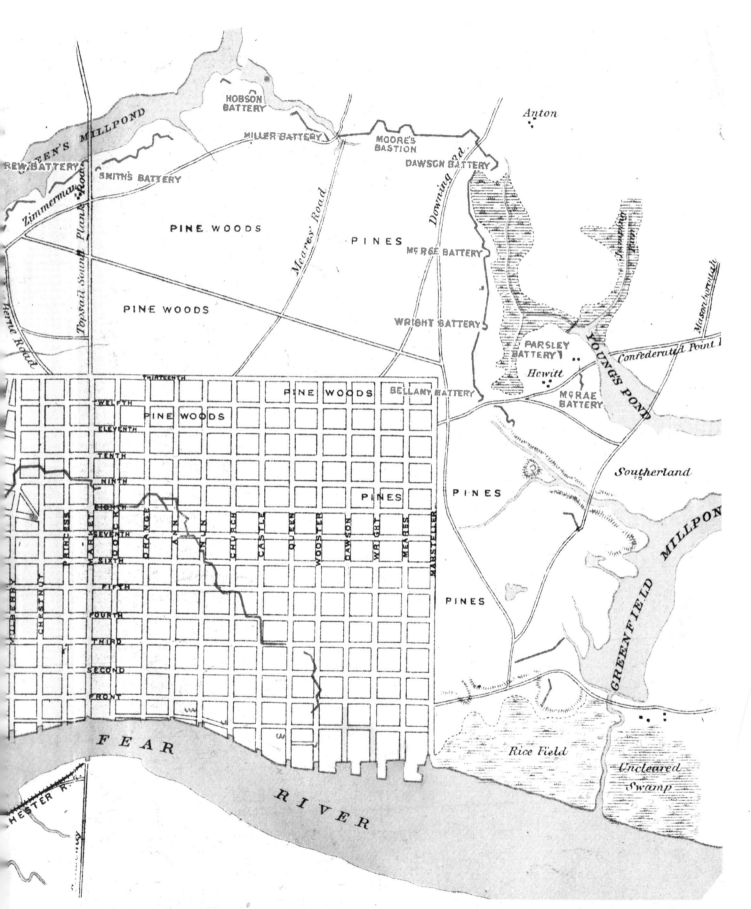

CHAPTER 2
RIVERFRONT

NHCPL

In the 1890's (above) it is hard to recognize the city we know today. The three story building left of center is the Custom House that was replaced by the Federal Building after 1915. The riverfront in 1915 (below) shows the Custom House at the right. The tall white building just to the left of it is the recently completed Trust Building that still stands at the corner of Front and Market Streets. At the center is the Southern Building that stood at Front and Chestnut. At the left is the building at Front and Grace that later became Efird's Department Store.

HEURING

RIVERFRONT

LCFHS

In the 1920's (above) the Federal Building was recently completed. To the left at the corner of Water and Princess, the five floor structure is the Maffit Building. The Murchison Bank Building, now the First Union Building, is at the left. At the far right is the ferry boat that was used to cross the river before the bridges were built.

LCFHS

Although the above and below pictures from the 1940's are similar, they are slightly different. The north side of Market Street (above) can clearly be seen as far as the First Baptist Church at the upper right. At the upper left (below) the northeastern part of the city is visible.

LCFHS

LCFHS

In about 1954 (above) the newly completely Belk Beery Department Store is at the upper center just to the right of the Cape Fear Hotel. The Fergus Ark Restaurant is the boat at the lower left. By the early 1960's (below) the white building at the lower right center is the Wachovia Bank. A parking lot in front of it has replaced the Maffit Building.

LCFHS

RIVERFRONT NORTH AREA

NHCPL

Looking to the northwest (above) in the 1930's, the bridges crossing the Cape Fear and Northeast Cape Fear Rivers that had been built in the late 1920's are at the upper left and upper right. The highly industrialized section of the city north of the downtown area (below) evolved at that location due to the presence of the railroad nearby. The roundhouse is at the upper right. The freight piers protruding into the river enabled inland rail freight to find access by ship to markets throughout the world.

NHCPL

LCFHS

Looking south (above) the railroad roundhouse is at the lower left. In the 1950's the number of rail freight cars right of center and the ships give an indication of the impact of the railroad on the economy. The small building shaped like a cube in the center is today's Railroad Museum. By the late 1960's (below) the railroad had departed. The newly completed parking deck is in the center and in front of it is the steel skeleton that would become the Hilton Hotel.

LCFHS

RIVERFRONT

LCFHS

Looking east in 1960 (above), the preparations for a berth for the *North Carolina* had not yet begun. The arrival in 1961 of the *North Carolina* (below) brightened the spirits of the city that had been saddened by the recent departure of the Atlantic Coast Line Railroad.

NHCPL

LCFHS

The Dram Tree (above) was located south of the city. A dram or drink was given to the sailors at this point as they entered or departed from the city. It may have been to Wilmington what the Statue of Liberty is to New York City. The tree was destroyed during World War I to build a shipyard. It is remembered (below) as a park just north of the Cape Fear Memorial Bridge.

KOEPPEL

RIVERFRONT

BRYANT

The Cape Fear River in the 1990's showing the downtown skyline.

LOWMAN

In the 1990's the view from the battleship to the beach gives an excellent indication of the size of our area.

CHAPTER 3

NORTH FRONT STREET
BETWEEN MARKET & PRINCESS

NHCPL

Looking north at Market Street (above) in about 1900. At the right William
Green and Co. and at the left Bellamy Drugs occupy the corner properties.
There were some changes (below) by 1945. The Trust Building stands where the
Green property was located. Right of center is the Bailey Theater. Although in
the same building, Toms Drug Co. has replaced Bellamy Drugs.

NHCPL

LOWMAN

In the 1990's the Masonic and First Union Buildings are still left of center and the corner buildings are essentially unchanged.

NORTH FRONT STREET
BETWEEN MARKET & PRINCESS

NHCPL

Looking north, the east side of North Front Street (above) is at mid-block in about 1900. The building on the right is the Purcell House Hotel built in 1874. It remained until the Bailey Theater replaced it in 1940. Although the Bailey Theater showed its last movie in 1980, the facade (below) remained in 1999.

LOWMAN

NORTH FRONT STREET
BETWEEN MARKET & PRINCESS

North Front Street, Wilmington, N. C.

NHCPL

Looking north from Market Street, the west side of North Front Street in 1900 (above) shows the Masonic Building at center, and the Purcell House Hotel is across the street. Right of center at the northwest corner of Princess Street is Peoples Bank. Looking south at Princess Street in 1999 (below), the Masonic Building is right of center.

LOWMAN

STREET NUMBERS
MARKET TO PRINCESS

These listings indicate the business or person occupying the street numbers for the years indicated. The even numbers are on the east side of the street and the odd numbers on the west. The numerical order proceeds from the south to the north.

Although an occupant may be shown at a certain number for the years 1920 - 1940, for example, they may not have been at this location for the first time in 1920 nor for the last time in 1940. Since the years indicated have been arbitrarily chosen, the purpose of this survey is only to show who was at a given number on North Front Street for a particular year. There is no intent to list every occupant of each address. If a number was unoccupied or didn't exist for the year chosen, then the year and/or the number is not shown.

It must be added that the city occasionally revised the numbering system of some of its blocks. In other words, number 205 in 1915 could become 211 in 1930 and 229 in 1940. The number indicated in these situations is the approximate one that would be in effect today.

1 - 3

1915 - 1920	Bellamy Drugs
1930	Speer Drugs
1940 - 1998	Toms Drugs

2 - 4

	Trust Building
1915 - 1920	Atlantic Trust & Banking
1950 - 1970	Berman Jewelers
1998	Phuza Juice

5

1915 - 1920	Mission Pharmacy
1930 - 1940	Andrew Pope Jewelry
1950 - 1970	Stanley's Jewelers
1990	Yogurt Etc.
1998	Port Hole Gift Shop

6

1920	The Center Market
1930	James Book Store
1940	O.H. Shoemaker Stationary

7

1915 - 1920	Boylan & Hancock
1930	Max Warshauer Dept. Store
1940	Sol Checkner WOMEN'S WEAR
1950 - 1960	Reeds Jewelers
1970	Love's Jewelers
1980	Stanley's Jewelers
1990	Gene Merritt Real Estate
1998	Port City Java

8

1920	The Center Market
1930	The Office Outfitter
1940	O.H. Shoemaker Stationary
1950	Cooperative Bank
1970 - 1990	First Citizens Bank & Trust
1998	The Town Creole Eatery

9

1920	J.M. Solky & Co.
1930	Charles Stieff, Inc.
1940 - 1980	Foy - Roe & Co. DEPARTMENT STORE
1998	Front Street Micro Brewery

10 - 12

1915 - 1930	George Honnet 1867 Jewelers
1940 - 1998	Kingoff Jewelers

11 - 13

1915 - 1970	S.H. Kress & Co. DEPARTMENT STORE
1980	Buy - Rite Discount Store
1990	U.S. Army Corps of Engineers

14

1915 - 1920	William Springer & Co.
1930	Gregg Brothers Hardware
1940 - 1960	George Honnet 1867 Jewelers
1970	Shain's Jewelers
1980	Big Ike's Shoe Repair

15

	Masonic Building

MARKET TO PRINCESS

16

1915 - 1920	Purcell House Hotel
1930	Purcell Furnished Rooms
1950	Kiddy Shop Clothing
1960	Lelia Corbin MILLINERY
1970	David's Hair Goods

18 - 20

1915 - 1930	Baxter Tobacco Co.
1940 - 1980	Bailey Theater

22

1915 - 1930	Royal Bakery
1950 - 1970	Mademoiselle Shop
1990	Third World Reflections Shop
1998	Daughtry's Antiques & Books

23 - 27

	Grand Building
1915 - 1920	Grand Theater
1930 - 1940	McLellan Stores

23 - 31

1950 - 1960	McLellan Stores

23

1990	Dynamic Fitness
1998	Artec of Carolinas Beauty Salon

24

1920 - 1930	Wilmington Cigar Co.
1940 - 1980	Freeman Shoe Co.
1990	Daughtry's Antiques & Books
1998	Nautical Hang Ups

26

1915	Southern Hotel
1920	Harold & Roberson
1930	Dixie Shoe Store

26 - 28

1940 - 1960	Crystal Restaurant

26

1970	Sun Finance & Loan
1980 - 1998	Friendly Wig Shop

27

1970 - 1998	Reeds Jewelers

28

1915	Yarborough & Williams
1920	Wilmington Tonsorial Parlor
1930	Allen Blake ELECTRICAL CONTRACTOR
1970	Mills Jewelers
1980 - 1998	Simeone Printing & Advertising

29

1915 - 1920	A.D. Brown Co., Inc.

30

1915 - 1920	Chestnut & Freeman
1930	Freeman Shoe Co.
1950 - 1960	Kinney Shoes
1970	Buy - Rite, Inc. Cosmetics
1980	Cloud Nine Shoes, Inc.
1990	Rare Cargo Imported Handicrafts
1998	About Time ANTIQUES

31

1920	Shrier & Solomon
1930 - 1940	Kinney Shoes

32

1915	Isaac Shrier MEN'S CLOTHES
1920	Northam's Books & Stationary
1930	Boylan Shoes
1940 - 1970	Thom McAn Shoes
1980 - 1998	Lenny's MEN'S CLOTHES

33

1915	Shrier & Solomon
1930	Anderson & Hufham Clothing
1940 - 1950	Wonder Dress Shop

34

1915	Woodall & Sheppard, Inc.
1920 - 1950	Isaac Shrier & Sons MEN'S CLOTHES
1960 - 1998	Su-Ann Shoes

35

1940	J.C. Anderson & Son MEN'S CLOTHES
1950	Art High Clothing Co.
1970	First National Bank of Eastern North Carolina
1980	Bank of North Carolina
1990	Peoples Bank & Trust
1998	Paleo Sun Cafe

CHAPTER 4

NORTH FRONT STREET
BETWEEN PRINCESS & CHESTNUT

NHCPL

In about 1925 the corner of Princess and North Front Street is in the foreground. The roof of the Masonic Building is on the left. Peoples Bank is at the lower center. The tall building with the flag is The Murchison National Bank. At the far right center is the tower of the old Post Office Building. The building with a steeple on the left side of the street in the distance is one of the offices of the Atlantic Coast Line Railroad Company.

NHCPL

Looking north (above) in about 1905, to the left of the trees at center is the Southern Building completed in 1904. The same location (below) circa 1940 illustrates the Murchison Building behind the Southern Building. The Bear Building is at the right corner.

LCFHS

LOWMAN

By 1999 (above) Wachovia Bank, completed in 1960, replaced People's Bank at the left. Isaac's is where the Bear Building was located.

NORTH FRONT STREET
BETWEEN PRINCESS & CHESTNUT

LCFHS

In about 1900 looking south (above) at mid-block, the Masonic Building is right of center. The Orton Hotel is at the right. The old Post Office is at the left (below) looking south near the corner of Chestnut Street in about 1930.

NHCPL

NHCPL

Just north of the corner of Chestnut Street (above) in 1925 looking south, the Home Savings Bank is on the left and the old Post Office is to its right. The Southern Building is across from it. The current Post Office (below left) was completed in 1936. Today the Bank of America stands where the Southern Building was located until 1957.

LOWMAN

STREET NUMBERS
NORTH FRONT BETWEEN PRINCESS & CHESTNUT

These listings indicate the business or person occupying the street numbers for the years indicated. The even numbers are on the east side of the street and the odd numbers on the west. The numerical order proceeds from the south to the north.

Although an occupant may be shown at a certain number for the years 1920 - 1940, for example, they may not have been at this location for the first time in 1920 nor for the last time in 1940. Since the years indicated have been arbitrarily chosen, the purpose of this survey is only to show who was at a given number on North Front Street for a particular year. There is no intent to list every occupant of each address. If a number was unoccupied or didn't exist for the year chosen, then the year and/or the number is not shown.

It must be added that the city occasionally revised the numbering system of some of its blocks. In other words, number 205 in 1915 could become 211 in 1930 and 229 in 1940. The number indicated in these situations is the approximate one that would be in effect today.

100 - 102
1915 - 1930	United Cigar Stores
1940	Style Booterie

100 - 104
1950 - 1970	Holly Shop WOMEN'S CLOTHES
1980	The Hustler MEN'S CLOTHES
1990 - 1998	Isaac's MEN'S CLOTHES

101 - 105
1915 - 1950	People's Savings Bank
1960 - 1998	Wachovia Bank

104
1915 - 1920	A.O. Schuster
1930	The Young Men's Clothes Shop
1940	Cinderella Booterie

105
1915 - 1940	Walker Taylor Insurance

106
1915 - 1920	Munson & Co.
1930 - 1940	Merit Shoe Co.

107
1915	The Gilberts
1920	Lenox Hotel
1930	Will Rehder Florist
1990	Sun Brokers

108
1915	George French & Sons Co.
1920	Rexall Drugs
1930 - 1940	Saunders Drugs
1950	Beverly's WOMEN'S CLOTHES
1960	Wonder Shop WOMEN'S CLOTHES
1970	Justin's WOMEN'S CLOTHES
1980	Jeans Glory
1990	Betty B's Antiques
1998	Cencio WOMEN'S CLOTHES

109
1915	Cape Fear Hardware
1920 - 1930	Liberty Clothing

110 - 112
1915 - 1930	F.W. Woolworth 5¢ & 10¢ Store

110 - 114
1940	F.W. Woolworth 5¢ & 10¢ Store

112
1950 - 1960	Merit Shoe Co.
1970	Country Vogue WOMEN'S CLOTHES
1980	Interstate Securities
1990	Country Vogue WOMEN'S CLOTHES
1998	Rare Cargo Apparel

NORTH FRONT BETWEEN PRINCESS & CHESTNUT

113
1915	Orton Confectionary
1920	Wilmington Cafe

114 - 116
1915 - 1920	Warren Cigar Stores
1930	Thom McAn Shoes

115 - 119
1915 - 1940	Orton Hotel

115 - 117
1950 - 1980	Diana Stores WOMEN'S CLOTHES
1990	Front Street Photography
1998	Blowing in The Wind HOBBY SHOP

116
1950	Saunders Drugs
1970 - 1980	Color Craft Camera Shop
1990	Cape Fear Camera
1998	Coastal Camera

117
1915	E.L. Mathews Candy
1920	Elvington Dependable Drugs
1930 - 1940	George Higgins Jewelry

119
1915	M.L. Jass
1920	Alma Brown
1930	William Kamer Optometrist
1940	Lee Welch
1950	The Jewel Box

121
1915	The Air Dome
1920 - 1940	Royal Theater
1950	Su-Ann Shoes
1990	Scandals Hair & Make-Up
1998	Don Tickle Imports

123
1950	Glen - More Clothing
1960 - 1970	Hufham's MENS STORE
1990	Shoe Doctor

127
1950 - 1970	Cinderella Booterie Shoes
1980	Justin's LADIES CLOTHES
1998	Unique Americana USED MERCHANDISE

130
1998	Fore - Play Travel Agency

131
1950-1960	Sher-Lynn Shoppe WOMEN'S CLOTHES
1970	Payne's Clothing
1980	Bryan's Formal Center MEN'S RENTALS
1990	Cape Fear Formal Wear

133
1950 - 1960	Jones Nixon Cigar Store
1970 - 1990	Orton Cigar Store
1998	Bessie's Bar

137
1950 - 1970	Orton Barber Shop

139
1950	Stein's Stores Clothing
1970 - 1990	Dennis' Jewel Box
1998	Fulton's Fuji Oriental Furniture

141
1950 - 1970	Sally's Frocks
1980 - 1998	Sally Shop

143
1960	My Shop WOMEN'S CLOTHES
1970 - 1980	Butler's Shoes
1990	Garrick's Carolina Office Supply
1998	Betty B's Antiques

151
1960	Butler's Shoes

152
1915 - 1998	Post Office

NORTH FRONT BETWEEN PRINCESS & CHESTNUT

155

1915	C.W. Polvogt Co.
1920	Bon Marche
1930	N. Jacobi Hardware
1940 - 1950	Will Rehder Florist
1960	Nesbet Young Miss Shop
1970	North Carolina National Bank
1980	Bank of North Carolina
1990	NCNB National Bank
1998	Nations Bank

157

1940	The Beautician Beauty Shop
1950 - 1960	Crawford's Fashion Center

161

	Southern Building 1915 - 1950
1915	Southern National Bank
1920	Citizens Bank
1930	Polly-Anna Beauty Shoppe
1940 - 1950	Vogue Beauty Shoppe

165

1930	David's Inc. CLOTHING
1940 - 1950	Julian Taylor MEN'S CLOTHING
1960	Nesbet's Women's Clothes

CHAPTER 5

NORTH FRONT STREET
BETWEEN CHESTNUT & GRACE

NHCPL

Looking north from the northeast corner of Chestnut Street (above) in about 1932, the building on the right had recently become the Morris Plan Bank. It had been the Home Savings Bank. Belk Williams is in the middle of the block and the sign for Efird's Department Store is at the corner of Grace Street. The first tall building in the distance is the Hotel Wilmington and Union Station protrudes behind it. In the 1990's (below) many of the buildings remain, but few occupants remain the same.

LOWMAN

NORTH FRONT STREET
BETWEEN CHESTNUT & GRACE

NHCPL

At mid-block (above) on the west side of the street in about 1900, the offices of the Seaboard Airline Railroad are on the left. To the left of the trolley at the corner of Grace Street is the YMCA. By the 1940's (below) the block had emerged as a major retail center. To the right of the street light pole, the hotel sign refers to the Brunswick Hotel that occupied the former YMCA building. Just beyond is Sears Roebuck in today's Cotton Exchange. The steeple at the far right is on one of the Atlantic Coast Line Railroad office buildings.

CF MUSEUM

NORTH FRONT STREET
BETWEEN CHESTNUT & GRACE

NHCPL

Looking south from southwest corner of Grace Street (above) in about 1900, the corner building was occupied by Bear Wholesale Dry Goods. At the far left is the Seaboard Airline Railroad office buildings. The Elks Temple Building is north of it. In 1999 (below) the building on the left was the location of Efird's Department Store. The Elks Temple building is still standing, and The First Union Building in the distance is at the northwest corner of Chestnut Street.

LOWMAN

STREET NUMBERS
NORTH FRONT BETWEEN CHESTNUT & GRACE

These listings indicate the business or person occupying the street numbers for the years indicated. The even numbers are on the east side of the street and the odd numbers on the west. The numerical order proceeds from the south to the north.

Although an occupant may be shown at a certain number for the years 1920 - 1940, for example, they may not have been at this location for the first time in 1920 nor for the last time in 1940. Since the years indicated have been arbitrarily chosen, the purpose of this survey is only to show who was at a given number on North Front Street for a particular year. There is no intent to list every occupant of each address. If a number was unoccupied or didn't exist for the year chosen, then the year and/or the number is not shown.

It must be added that the city occasionally revised the numbering system of some of its blocks. In other words, number 205 in 1915 could become 211 in 1930 and 229 in 1940. The number indicated in these situations is the approximate one that would be in effect today.

200
1915-1920	Home Savings Bank
1930-1940	Morris Plan Bank
1950-1960	Bank of Wilmington
1970	First Union National Bank
1998	Robert & Patricia DeYoung

201
	Murchison Building
1915-1920	Murchison National Bank
1930	North Carolina Bank & Trust
1940 - 1950	Beulah Meier Dress Shop
1960 - 1970	Huggins Jewelers
1980 - 1998	First Union National Bank

202
1915 - 1920	Peterson and Rulfs Shoes
1930	Gross Millinery
1960	Reed's Millinery

204
	Peterson - Rulf's Building
1915	DuBois Laboratory
1920	U.S. Navy Recruiting
1950	Wilmington Smart & Thrifty Dresses

205
1940 - 1950	Security National Bank
1940 - 1970	Murchison Soda Shop
1980	WCM, Inc.
1990 - 1998	Pender's Luncheonette

206
1950 - 1960	Cannon Shoe Store

207
1970 - 1980	Burnell Curtis Optometrist

208
1940 - 1950	Reed's Millinery
1970	Wilmington Optical Center
1998	Imperial Trading

209
1940 - 1970	Wilmington Star News

210
1998	Layne & Nancy Barbers

212
1940	Smart & Thrifty Dresses
1960 - 1970	Gurr Jewelers
1998	Screen Play Video

213
1930 - 1970	Standard Pharmacy
1950	The Children's Shop

214
1940	Cannon Shoe Store
1950	Wahl's Department Store

216
1980	Century Men's Shop
1990 - 1998	New Element Art Gallery

NORTH FRONT BETWEEN CHESTNUT & GRACE

217
1940	William Kamer Optometrist
1950	Wm. Kamer-Burnell Curtis Opt.
1960	Burnell Curtis Optometrist

218 - 220
1940	City Optical Company
1950	City Optical Company

219
1930	City Optical Company
1930 - 1940	Albert Gibson's MEN'S CLOTHES
1950	Gibson's Haberdasher
1960	American Banker's Insurance

220
1930	G. Dannenbaum WOMEN'S CLOTHES
1980	Barclays American Financial
1990	Bus. Intelligent Terminal Computers
1998	Sentimental Journey Antiques

221
	Bulluck Building
1930 - 1950	Bulluck Hospital
1960 - 1970	Coastal Plain Life Insurance
1990 - 1998	Comprehensive Home Health Care

223
1940	Lewis J. Stein MEN'S CLOTHES
1950 - 1990	Ed Fleischman & Bros. MEN'S CLOTHES

224
1915	American National Bank
1930 - 1950	Wilmington Furniture Storage
1960 - 1970	Stelen's, Inc. WOMEN'S CLOTHES
1980	Wise Fashions
1990	Cape Fear United Way
1998	Shaw University

226
1915	Gaylord's DEPARTMENT STORE
1920 - 1930	Belk Williams DEPARTMENT STORE
1960 - 1970	Wahlgreen's Drug Store

226 - 246
1940	Belk Williams DEPARTMENT STORE

226 - 248
1950	Belk Williams DEPARTMENT STORE

227
1920	Wilmington Shoe Company
1930	The Music Shop/Speer Drugs
1940	Bijou Sweet Shop

228
1960	Robinson's Stores WOMEN'S CLOTHES
1970	Wonder Shop, Inc. WOMEN'S CLOTHES
1980 - 1998	Glasgow Hicks Insurance

229 - 233
1915 - 1950	Bijou Theater

230
1915	Coast Line Hotel
1915 - 1920	People's Supply

232
1960	Wahl's Department Store

233
1915 - 1920	Eagle's Club
1920	Automobile Supply Company

236
1915	Coast Line Cafe
1920	Wilmington Furniture Co.

237
1915 - 1920	Star Cafe
1930 - 1950	Western Union

243
1930 - 1970	J.C. Penney
1990 - 1998	McKim & Creed Engineers

245
1990	A.G. Edwards & Son

246
1930	Miller's Quality Shop

247
1920	Camera Shop/T.A.&F.S. Sheperd
1940	Sally's Frocks

NORTH FRONT BETWEEN CHESTNUT & GRACE

248
1940	Wahl's Fashionland WOMENS CLOTHES
1970	Scottie's Drug
1990	Talbert Cox & Associates
1998	The Camel's Eye/Network R.E.

249
1915	Western Union
1920 - 1960	Saffo's Restaurant
1970	The Earl of Sandwich Shop
1980 - 1998	New Liverpool Restaurant

250
1915 - 1920	The A. David Co. / Moose Club
1930	Hattie Schiller Millinery
1940	Su-Ann Shoes

251
1915	Gray & Company
1920	Fleischmann Co. / J.W. Plummer
1930	Askin's Clothiers
1950	Larkin's Clothes
1960 - 1998	Arnold Sobol Optometrist

252
1915	M. Rosenmann & Son

254 - 262
1915 - 1920	Bluethenthal Co.
1930	F&W Grand Silver 5&10¢ Store
1940 - 1960	H.L. Green Co. Dept. Store
1970	McCrory's Department Store
1998	Warwick's & Associates / Radio Station WHQR

255
	Elks Temple Building
1915 - 1940	Elks Home
1960	The Children's Shop

257
1915	Hyman Supply Company
1920	Hyman Supply Company / Kelly Springfield Tires
1930 - 1950	Peoples Furniture
1960 - 1970	City Optical Company

259
1915	Wilmington Shoe Company / Postal Tel Cable
1920	Williams Brothers

261
1915	Fleischmann Co. / JW Plummer
1920	Postal Tel Cable
1930 - 1950	Hyman Supply Co.
1960 - 1970	Shoemakers Office Supply Co.
1990	Fountaine Bridals / Southern Accents Florist
1998	United Cerebral Palsy Center

263
1920	Crescent Candy Co.
1930	Cox & Co. Milliners / Little Art Shop

264
1940	Hattie Schiller Millinery
1950	Gurr Jewelers
1960 - 1970	Don Whittemore Optometrist

265
1998	Jim Brannock / Joseph Sanger

267
1940	Spor-Tee Shop Woman's Wear
1950	Marian's Dress Shop

271
1930 - 1940	Postal Tel Cable Company
1950 - 1970	Singer Sewing Machine Co.
1980	The Orange Peel
1990	Susie's World of Dolls
1998	The Retro Room

272 - 276
1915 - 1920	Einstein Bros. Department Store
1930 - 1970	Efird's Department Store

273
1930	Crescent Candy Company / Ladies Dress Shop
1940	JayDee WOMEN'S CLOTHES
1960	Hufham's Clothes
1980 - 1998	City Opticians

275
1915	Gustave Dannebaum / Post Dater Stamp Co.
1970 - 1980	Household Finance Co.

277
1915	Bunting Hicks Drug / Wilmington Homestead & Loan
1940 - 1990	Julia Shop WOMEN'S CLOTHES
1998	Chadsworth Columns

CHAPTER 6
NORTH FRONT STREET
BETWEEN GRACE & RED CROSS

LCFHS

In the 1940's (above) the corner of Grace Street is in the foreground. Efird's Department Store is at the southeast corner and H.L. Green & Co. is at the lower right. Just beyond the Esso sign at the center is the Hotel Wilmington. Union Station is at the northeast corner of Red Cross St. at the top left of center. The steeple at the upper left is part of an Atlantic Coast Line Railroad office building. In the 1990's (below) the foreground is mid-block between Walnut and Red Cross Streets. At the left is a Cape Fear Community College building. No buildings are present where the Hotel Wilmington and Union Station once stood. The Police Department is on the right.

LOWMAN

NORTH FRONT STREET
BETWEEN GRACE & RED CROSS

NHCPL

At the southeast corner of Red Cross Street (above) in about 1900, The Atlantic Hotel, originally called The Railroad Hotel, was across the street from Union Station. By the 1960's (below) the building no longer retained the wood design that had been at the upper portion of the facade. People's Furniture, now on South College Road, had replaced the private home that had been to the right of the building. Hotel Wilmington is at the right at the southeast corner of Walnut Street.

CF MUSEUM

NHCPL

At the northeast corner of Walnut Street, Alexander Sprunt & Son, cotton exporters, located their new offices (above) in the 1880's. The land became available after the Front Street Methodist Church was destroyed by fire. By the 1920's the business relocated to the southwest corner of Walnut Street. Today (below) this building is part of the Cotton Exchange. The First Union Building is at the left at the corner of Chestnut Street.

LOWMAN

LOWMAN

Today Cape Fear Community College (above) is at the northeast corner of Front & Walnut Streets.

NORTH FRONT STREET
BETWEEN GRACE & RED CROSS

NHCPL

Looking north just south of Walnut Street (above) in about 1916, the Hotel Wilmington on the right was new. The Atlantic Coast Line Railroad office building with the steeple, on the left, had been built in the 1880's and it was demolished in 1962. The white structure crossing North Front Street in the distance was an elevated walkway connecting Union Station to railroad offices. In the 1990's Cape Fear Community College (below) has buildings on both sides of the block between Walnut and Red Cross streets.

LOWMAN

STREET NUMBERS
NORTH FRONT BETWEEN GRACE & RED CROSS

These listings indicate the business or person occupying the street numbers for the years indicated. The even numbers are on the east side of the street and the odd numbers on the west. The numerical order proceeds from the south to the north.

Although an occupant may be shown at a certain number for the years 1920 - 1940, for example, they may not have been at this location for the first time in 1920 nor for the last time in 1940. Since the years indicated have been arbitrarily chosen, the purpose of this survey is only to show who was at a given number on North Front Street for a particular year. There is no intent to list every occupant of each address. If a number was unoccupied or didn't exist for the year chosen, then the year and/or the number is not shown.

It must be added that the city occasionally revised the numbering system of some of its blocks. In other words, number 205 in 1915 could become 211 in 1930 and 229 in 1940. The number indicated in these situations is the approximate one that would be in effect today.

300

1930	Kingoff Jewelers
1940	LaMode Deluxe Shoppe WOMEN'S WEAR
1950 - 1980	Camera Shop
1998	General Assembly Coffee Shop

301

1915 - 1920	National Woolen Mills
1930 - 1940	Camera Shop
1950	Harrill Music Store

302

1915 - 1920	S.P. Collier
1930	McGrath & Co. Music
1940	Edwin Farrell & Co. Furniture
1998	Butte's Antiques

303

1915	Imperial Hotel
1920	Carolina Hotel
1930 - 1950	Brunswick Hotel
1960	Plisco Furniture Co.

304

1930	Harry's Exclusive Ladies Shop
1940	Singer Sewing Machine Co.
1950	Nesbit's Ladies Shop
1998	Beverage Boutique

305

1915	Atlantic Barber Shop
1920	Standard Supply Co.
1930	Mae Frink Dressmaker / Service News

1940	Conrad Wessell Refrigerators
1950	Roxy Restaurant

306

1940	Harry Payne & Son News Dealers
1950	B&H Hot Shoppe Restaurant
1960	Jiffy Grill Restaurant
1998	Suzanne Collins Moss Design Studio/ Elizabeth Messick Interiors/ Provenance Antique & Interiors

307

1920	Olympic Cafe

307-309

1930 - 1960	Sears, Roebuck & Co.

307

1990	Cotton Exchange
1998	Makado Gallery / R. Bryan Clothes

308

1915	Mrs. M.L. Willis / G.J. Vybel
1920	Mrs. L.C. Moore
1930 - 1940	Olympic Cafe
1950 - 1960	Mayflower Grill Restaurant

309

1915	Price Brothers / F.N. Finks / J.B. Avent
1920	Price Brothers / Martin O'Brien
1990	United Agencies Insurance
1998	Candy Barrel / Kitchen Shoppe UCB Insurance Center

NORTH FRONT BETWEEN GRACE & RED CROSS

310

1915	J.C. McCartney & Son / Meiers Marble & Granite Works
1920	H.J. McCartney Meier & O'Neal Brothers
1930 - 1950	Sutton - Council Furniture
1960 - 1970	Rhodes Furniture
1980	Hercofina Chemicals
1998	Block, Crouch, Keeter, Huffman / Cape Fear Book & Supply / Mailboxes

311

1915 - 1950	Samuel Bear & Sons WHOLESALE GROCERS
1950 - 1960	Firestone Auto Supplies
1998	City Zoo Gift Shop

311 - 313

1960 - 1970	Sutton-Council Furniture

312

1930	Pioneer Service Station

312 - 314

1940 - 1950	Morris & Motte Filling Station
1960	Carroll's Pure Oil Service Station

313

1915	Merrick Winslow Barber
1920	W.H. McEachern
1930	Standard Furniture Co.
1940	E.C. Moore & Co. Wholesale Notions

313 - 325

1980	Cotton Exchange

313

1990	Cape Fear Council of Governments
1998	Atlantic Brokerage / Full Web Properties Harbour Associates / The Nature Conservancy

314

1915	LeGwin Printing
1915 - 1920	Mrs. R.I. Morrison
1930	Mrs. Nannie Currie
1950	Shaw Paint & Wallpaper
1960	Evans Studio Photography

315

1915	Ye Lee

1920 - 1960	Merrick Winslow Barber
1920 - 1940	Harry Mosias Tailor
1950	Wilmington Post 9751 (VFW)
1998	M. Clothing WOMEN'S CLOTHES

316

1915	F.W. Jones
1920	Hotel Wilmington - Sample Room
1950	Goldcraft Studio Photographers
1998	Whittlers Bench Gift Shop

317

1915	F.W. Mohr
1920 - 1930	California Laundry

317 - 319

1940 - 1960	T.W. Wood & Sons Seeds

317

1970	Sutton-Council Furniture Showroom

318

1915 - 1960	Hotel Wilmington
1915	Harriss Typewriter & Advertising
1930	Radio Station WRBT
1960 - 1970	Western Union Telegraph

319

1930	Quality Cleaners and Taylors

319 - 321

1930 - 1950	Alexander Sprunt & Sons Cotton Exporters
1930	British Consulate / Lloyd's Insurance
1940	Champion Compress & Warehouse

319

1990	Sun Galleries Art Dealers

320

1998	Bear Mountain Hobby Shop

321

1960 - 1970	USO YMCA Club
1990 - 1998	Cotton Exchange Exec. Office
1998	Bullock & Whaley Real Estate / Screen Actors Guild / Laura Padgett Insurance

323

1915	Hotel Wilmington Sample Room
1920	Hotel Wilmington Paint Shop

325

1980	Cotton Exchange

NORTH FRONT BETWEEN GRACE & RED CROSS

400

1915 - 1920	Alexander Sprunt & Son
1920	British Ministry of Shipping/ Lloyds Insurance
1930	Carr, Poisson & James Lawyers
1940	Works Progress Administration (District Office)

400

1950	Carolina Milk Bar Restaurant
1960	Carolina Grill & Bar
1970	Parker Seed Co.

401

1915 - 1930	Jurgen Haar Grocer
1940	Home Grocery
1950	John Moscoves
1960	Southern Grill & Billiard

402

1915	A.J. Johnston
1920	Isaac Loewenthal
1930	Eliza Devine Antiques
1940	Quality Cleaners & Hatters
1950	Rainbow Grill Restaurant
1960	S&W Grill Restaurant
1980 - 1990	Carolina Power & Light

403

1915 - 1930	Coast Line Confectionary
1940	Coast Line Soda Shop
1950	Coast Line Cafe
1960	Top's Grill & Bar

404

1915	C.H. Daniels
1920	Land's Novelty Store
1930	E.C. Moore & Co. Notions
1940	Cinderella Beauty Shoppe
1950	Stanland's Shoe Store

405

1960	Nicholas Johnson

406

1915	Mrs. J.B. Parker
1920	American Cafe
1930 - 1950	Boston Lunch

408

1915	W.C. & Evelyn Capps

1920	Ideal Confection
1940 - 1960	California Laundry

410

1915	C.A. & Georgie Ulmer

411

1970 - 1980	Cape Fear Technical Institute
1990 - 1998	Cape Fear Community College

412

1915	Bryan & DeRose
1930	Pinehurst Miniature Golf
1960	Rhodes Warehouse

414

1915	Southern Express
1920	American Railway Express
1930	Railway Express
1940	Works Progress Admin. Handicraft Shop

415

1930 - 1960	Atlantic Coastline Railroad

416

1915	Southern Hat Co.
1930	Pender Furniture Co.
1940	Murray's Transfer Co.
1950	Shepard's Billiard Parlor/ Wilmington Lodge #343 (LOOM)
1960 - 1970	People's Furniture

416 - 418

1920	E.L. Mathews Candy Co.

418

1915	C.W. Nixon
1930	Gardner Coal Co. / Murray's Transfer
1940 - 1950	Atlantic Coast Line Employees Credit Union
1950	Howard's Radio Shop

418 - 420

1960	Godwin's Grill Restaurant

420

1915 - 1920	Atlantic Inn
1930	Atlantic Restaurant
1940	Carolina Cafe / Hotel
1950	A&M Grill / Xanthos Furnished Rooms
1970	Top's Grill & Bar

CHAPTER 7

SOUTH FRONT STREET

NHCPL

Looking north (above) from the middle of the block between Dock and Market Streets in about 1925, the Trust Building is the tallest structure on the right. The Masonic Building with the sloping roof appears to be opposite it, and the Murchison Building (with the flag) is in the distance. Looking south in the 1990's is the intersection (below) of Market and Front Streets. Finkelstein's Music Store is on the right and has been at this location since 1906.

LOWMAN

LCFHS

Looking north (above) just south of Dock Street in about 1920, a parade is about to commence. The Acme Saloon is on the right. The Seaman Bethel Building (on the far left) was destroyed in a 1955 fire. Today The Reel Cafe is at this location. In the 1990's (below), Roudabush Seed Company has replaced the Acme Saloon, and an empty lot is present where the building on the northwest corner had been.

LOWMAN

SOUTH FRONT STREET

NHCPL

Muter's Alley, the street at left (above), in about 1938, is between Dock and Orange Streets. The Kress sign at the upper right on the Masonic Building indicates where that store was located. There is no sign (below) on that building in the 1990's.

KOEPPEL

The intersection of Orange Street (above) looking north in about 1925 has Germania Hall on the right. This social center for people of German ancestry was demolished in about 1940. The building at the northwest corner (below) has awnings on the side as well as the front in the 1990's. A parking lot (bottom) has replaced Germania Hall.

SOUTH FRONT STREET

Looking north from the northwest corner of Orange Street (above) in about 1925, the Trust Building is in the center in the distance. The same location (below) circa 1940 indicated that the trolley tracks had recently been removed and buses were present.

In the 1990's (above) trees are on both sides of the street and many of the older buildings remain.

CHAPTER 8

MARKET STREET BETWEEN WATER & FRONT STREETS

NHCPL

Looking east from Water Street in the 1890's (above), with the exception of The First Baptist Church at the upper left and St. James at the upper right, there are few recognizable buildings. In the 1990's (below), the tree lined center mall has enhanced the street. The Federal Building is on the left, and Roy's Riverboat Landing Restaurant is on the right.

LOWMAN

MARKET STREET BETWEEN WATER & FRONT STREETS

NHCPL

In the 1890's looking west towards the river (above), Robert Bellamy Drugs is on the right at the corner of Front Street. Toms Drug Co. (below) replaced Bellamy in the 1930's. A slight outline of the circle that said M. W. Divine in the 1890's can still be seen today on the building behind Toms Drug Co.

LOWMAN

MARKET STREET BETWEEN WATER & FRONT STREETS

Looking south from the northwest corner of Front & Market Street (above) in the 1920's, there are several clothiers. In the 1990's (below) the buildings are the same although they have had some some alterations to the facades near the roof.

CHAPTER 9
MARKET STREET
BETWEEN FRONT & SECOND STREETS

The intersection of Front Street (above) is in the foreground in the 1890's. The steeple of First Baptist Church is left of center and St. James Church is right of center. By the 1920's (below) traffic congestion had begun.

The buildings at the corners (above) have not changed since the 1920's, but trees are enhancing the block in the 1990's.

LCFHS

The northwest corner of Second Street in the 1920's (above) includes the Groceteria where the 1990's Rhinoceros Club is located. This building had been the meeting place of the Masons before the Masonic Building had been completed in 1899. The building to the right of it was the Victoria Theater until 1934, the Carolina 1934-1953, and the Colony 1953-1974. It was demolished in 1976. The Rhinoceros Club (below) with the awning is the closest structure to the corner in the 1990's. The Trust Building is on the upper left and the First Union Building is at the upper right.

KOEPPEL

CHAPTER 10

MARKET STREET BETWEEN SECOND & FOURTH

NHCPL

Looking east in the 1920's (above), Second Street is in the right foreground. Market Street is in the center. The Burgwin / Wright House is right of center with the upper and lower porch. It was British General Cornwallis' headquarters during the Revolutionary War. St. James Church is behind it on Third Street, and the Colonial Apartments are to the left. By the 1990's the two buildings that were on the southeast corner of Market and Second Streets (below) were no longer standing. The top of St. James Church is at the left and the steeple of the First Presbyterian Church is right of center.

LOWMAN

NHCPL

In about 1915 looking east just west of the intersection of Third and Market Streets (above), the deRosset House with the white columned porch is on the left. It is on the northwest corner and was Confederate Headquarters. To the right of it are the Colonial Apartments, the YMCA, and the steeple of the First Baptist Church. The monument to Confederate Attorney General George Davis is in the center of the street. The intersection in the 1990's (below) has a parking lot where the Colonial Apartments and YMCA once stood. The First Citizens Bank has the white steeple on its roof at the left. St. James Church is on the right.

LOWMAN

MARKET STREET BETWEEN
SECOND & FOURTH STREETS

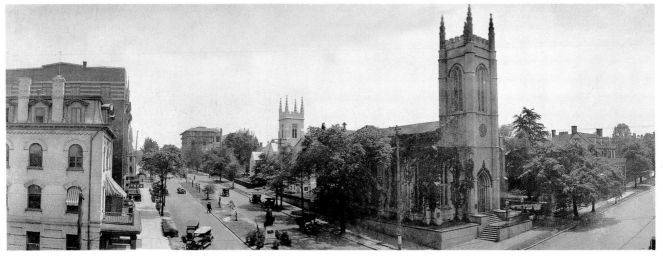

LCFHS

The southeastern corner of Third and Market Streets is in the foreground (above) in the 1920's. St. James Church is on the corner with the vestry building behind it. The Wootten House on the far right was no longer there after the early 1950's. Left of center in the distance are the Carolina Apartments. On the far left are the Colonial Apartments, and the YMCA is behind them.

MARKET STREET BETWEEN
SECOND & FOURTH STREETS

NHCPL

Looking west just beyond the corner of Third Street (above) in about 1900, on the right is the Potter House where Henry Clay made a speech in 1841. This house is on the left (below) in the 1920's. The deRosset house is to its right at the corner of Third Street. The YMCA is the building with the white stripes and Dr. Cranmer's house is at the right.

NHCPL

LOWMAN

The deRosset House has been replaced by Harold W. Wells & Son (above) in the 1990's. The Trust Building is at the left and the Rhinoceros Club and the Masonic Building are to its right.

CHAPTER 11

MARKET STREET
BETWEEN FOURTH & SIXTH

NHCPL

Looking east at Fourth Street in about 1920 (above), the Beery House is on the left and Wilmington Light Infantry is to its right. The First Baptist Church is left of center opposite the Carolina Apartments at the corner of Fifth Avenue. The Cornelius Harnett Monument in center foreground honors a member of the Continental Congress. Temple of Israel is at the right. The Sheriff's Department Building (below) on the left was built in the late 1970's. Few other changes had occurred by the 1990's.

LOWMAN

LCFHS

The Beery House (above) in the 1920's on the left stood at the northeast corner of Fourth Street until about 1950. Wilmington Light Infantry at the right was built as a private home by John Taylor in 1847. The Light Infantry occupied it from 1892 - 1951. It was the location of the library from 1956 - 1981, when the library relocated to Chestnut Street. In the late 1970's the Sheriff's Department (below) at the left occupied the former Beery House site.

KOEPPEL

MARKET STREET BETWEEN FOURTH & SIXTH STREETS

NHCPL

The northeast corner of Fifth Avenue has been the location of John Bellamy's home (above) since 1857. It is now open to the public. In the 1900's his son Robert lived in the house to the right. It had been built in the 1890's and was destroyed by fire in the 1980's. St. Paul's Lutheran Church is at the right. The Kenan Fountain (below) was placed at the intersection in 1921 as well as the bench at the center mall.

LOWMAN

CHAPTER 12

WATER STREET

NHCPL

At the foot of Market Street in about 1900 (above), the large number of boats indicates a high level of commercial activity. The building with two chimneys at the upper right is the Custom House. It was replaced by the existing Federal Building (below) after 1915. The excursion boat at the left traveled to Southport. Note the tracks for freight trains in front of the Federal Building.

NHCPL

By the 1990's (right) with the addition of trees and the railroad tracks removed, the area's appearance is enhanced for the enjoyment of tourists.

LOWMAN

WATER STREET

Looking north at the corner of Princess Street in about 1940 (above), the river can not be seen on the left due to the large number of commercial buildings. In the 1990's the parking deck built in 1966 (below) replaced the buildings on the east side of the street. Trees are between the street and the river on the west. The First Union Building is at the upper right.

RIVENBARK

Looking south just north of Chestnut Street in about 1958 (above), the building in the distance on the right is at the foot of Market Street. The building right of center with the white bricks extending to the height of the first floor is J.W. Murchison Hardware Company at the corner of Chestnut Street. The parking deck (below) was built on the east side of Water Street in the 1960's after the commercial buildings formerly located there were razed.

KOEPPEL

WATER STREET

NHCPL

The intersection with Nun Street (above) in about 1900 is on the other side of the wooden gate at the right. The wharf that extends from Water Street to the river accommodated ships that would transport barrels of tar, resin and turpentine to many parts of the world. The city's downtown waterfront is in the distance. The Masonic Building is to the right of the two chimneys right of upper center. The tower of the old Post Office is right of the Masonic building, and the steeple of the New Hanover County Courthouse is right of that. The Pilot House Restaurant (below) is now located in the building whose roof is visible just beyond the above mentioned wharf.

LOWMAN

NHCPL

The northeast corner of Ann Street (above) was the location of W.B. Thorpe & Co. in the 1920's. In the 1990's (below) this area is called Chandler's Wharf and has a number of stores located within it. Although the second floor at the right side of the building is no longer present, the balance of it has become a popular area for shoppers.

LOWMAN

WATER STREET

NHCPL

South of Dock Street looking north in about 1940 a freight car (above) is at the end of the tracks. To the left of it is the J.W. Brooks Wholesale Grocery building. The man with the bottlenosed dolphin at the left was not necessarily the one who caught it. In the 1990's (below) the Brooks building is left of the tree. It has been recently converted to apartments. The building at the right seems to be improving with age. The open area just beyond it was formerly the location of the Ice House Restaurant.

LOWMAN

THIRD STREET

At the northeast corner of Market Street (above) in about 1910, the Colonial Hotel later became an apartment house. It was destroyed by fire in 1962. The 1892 New Hanover County Courthouse is to the left and City Hall is just beyond. A parking lot (below) is located on the corner in the 1990's.

THIRD STREET

CAPE FEAR MUSEUM

The northwest corner of Princess Street (above) was the location of the Odd Fellows Building until the late 1960's. In the 1990's (below) Centura Bank on the left and BB&T behind it occupy this area.

LOWMAN

NHCPL

Looking south near the southeast corner of Chestnut Street (above) in about 1918, City Hall is on the left. The New Hanover County Courthouse is behind it at the corner of Princess Street. The other buildings beyond can be seen in the following sequence: the Colonial Hotel, St. James Church, the Wootten House and the steeple of the First Presbyterian Church. In the 1990's (below), the Wootten House and Colonial Hotel are no longer present.

LOWMAN

THIRD STREET

CAPE FEAR MUSEUM

In about 1930 (above) there were few parking spaces near the New Hanover County Courthouse at the southeast corner of Princess Street. The Colonial Apartments and St. James Church are on the right. The absence of Colonial Apartments (below) is the most significant structural change in the 1990's.

LOWMAN

RIVENBARK

The Azalea Festival has been an important event since the late 1940's. In the early 1950's (above) a special camera technique gives the impression that Third Street has a bend in it. The MacMillan and Cameron service station is in the center foreground and Belk Beery is to the right where the library is located in the 1990's. City Hall is at the left and the New Hanover County Courthouse is behind it. From the northwest corner of Market Street in the 1990's (below) looking north, the size of the crowd has not diminished. Harold Wells & Son occupies the corner and the Gore Building is to its right. The Wallace building, Centura Bank and BB&T are the three most prominent buildings to the north in that order. At the upper left is the Wachovia Bank with the First Union Building to its right and Cape Fear Apartments at upper center.

WELLS

CHAPTER 14

PRINCESS STREET

NHCPL

Looking east in 1911 where Princess Street begins at the intersection with Water Street (above), the Maffitt building is on the left. When the Wachovia Bank building (below) was built in 1960, the Maffitt building was demolished and the land became a parking lot. The Federal Building is on the right.

LOWMAN

NHCPL

At the intersection of North Front Street in about 1920 (above) looking east, the sign at the right indicates a trolley going to Wrightsville Beach will stop there. The Wilmington Savings & Trust Company building is behind the left side of the sign. The tall building on the right was called the Garrell Building. It was built at the corner of Second Street in about 1910 and was destroyed in a 1973 fire. In the 1990's (below) the same building is still standing on the corner at the right, but some cosmetic changes have occurred. The top of the old County Courthouse can be seen in the distance to the right of center.

LOWMAN

PRINCESS STREET

NHCPL

Just east of the intersection with Second Street (above) in about 1912 looking west, the Garrell Building is the tallest structure on the left. On the opposite corner is the telephone company headquarters that in the 1990's still has Southern Bell Telephone written on its upper facade. The Wachovia Bank (below) is right of center in the distance.

LOWMAN

PRINCESS STREET

NHCPL

Looking west at the intersection of Third Street (above) in 1901, Orrell's Stable is on the left. The Odd Fellows Building is at the right. This area has a different appearance in the 1990's. The Wallace Building (below) was built in the 1920's where the stable had been. Centura Bank occupies the place where the Odd Fellows building stood until the late 1960's.

LOWMAN

Wilmington Then and Now

73

CHAPTER 15

RAILROAD /
CAPE FEAR COMMUNITY COLLEGE

NHCPL

The above station served the city at Red Cross and North Front Streets until 1912. The bridge that crossed the tracks on North Front Street before the concourse was built in 1913 is below. At the upper right is the cover above the tracks where passenger trains arrived and departed.

NHCPL

LCFHS

This aerial view shows the extent of the railroad complex. Nutt Street is at the left. North Front Street is just left of center, and Red Cross Street runs from North Front Street to the east and west. The lettered buildings are indicated below.

A&B- Atlantic Coast Line general offices.

C- Union Station with offices on upper floors.

D- Additional railroad offices, now a police station.

E- Storage of railroad records.

F- Concourse leading from station to trains.

G- Building to repair trains.

H- Roundhouse for trains.

NHCPL

Union Station is shown in 1920 with Red Cross Street in the foreground and North Front Street to the left. It was in use from 1913 until the railroad departed in the 1960's. It was a great architectural loss when it was demolished in 1970. Below is the area as it appears today with the Police Department at the right.

LOWMAN

LOWMAN

Just to the left of the windows closest to the front of today's Police Department are bricks below the white markings that indicate where the corridor existed that connected the building to the railroad station.

NHCPL

When travelers arrived or departed from trains they could see some of the city's beautiful flowers. The east side of the passenger train area furthest from the station is below.

NHCPL

RAILROAD / CAPE FEAR COMMUNITY COLLEGE

Wilmington, N.C., Atlantic Coast Line, General Offices.

NHCPL

Building "A" (above) was completed in 1889 and destroyed in 1962. It was on the west side of North Front Street between Walnut and Red Cross Streets. Today Cape Fear Community College is at this location (below).

LOWMAN

RAILROAD / CAPE FEAR COMMUNITY COLLEGE

Union Station is above at the right and building "B" is at the left. North Front Street is in the center and Red Cross Street is in the foreground. Today, as indicated below, it is difficult to believe this is the same place.

RAILROAD / CAPE FEAR COMMUNITY COLLEGE

NHCPL

Looking west from the North Front Street bridge (above), the freight office, today's Railroad Museum, is at the upper left and the Cape Fear River is beyond it. In a closer view (below), Nutt Street (with a watchman's shelter at the right), crosses the railroad tracks.

NHCPL

LOWMAN

Today the Railroad Museum is at the left, and The Coastline Inn is in the center. In front of it is a parking area where railroad tracks were, and the former freight buildings are now The Coastline Convention Center.

CHAPTER 16

POST OFFICE

NHCPL

Completed in 1889 at the southeast corner of North Front Street and Chestnut, its destruction in 1936 is arguably the greatest architectural loss the city has ever suffered. Although some people called for its preservation, those who demanded that unemployed people be given an opportunity to engage in demolition work prevailed since this occurred during the depths of the Depression.

NHCPL

POST OFFICE

NHCPL

The area behind the Post Office was called the City Park. Today, as indicated below, parking is needed at this location for postal vehicles. The former Cape Fear Hotel is at the right and the First Union Building is in the center.

NHCPL

LCFHS

The above Post Office that was built in 1936 continues to serve as the main U.S. Postal Service facility.

CHAPTER 17
CHURCHES

LCFHS

With South Third Street in the foreground and the corner of Market Street at the lower left, Wilmington looks like a city of churches. St. James Episcopal Church is at the corner followed by the Temple of Israel at Fourth Street and the Carolina Apartments behind it on Fifth Avenue. Across Market Street, to the left of St. James is the First Citizens Bank. The Sheriff's Department is on the corner of Fourth Street followed by Wilmington Light Infantry and the First Baptist Church at the corner of Fifth Avenue. The steeple of St. Paul's Evangelical Lutheran Church is beyond it at Sixth Street in the distance.

CHURCHES
ST. JAMES EPISCOPAL CHURCH

NHCPL

Completed in 1769, the above church was replaced by the church below after 1839. Both were built at the southeast corner of Third and Market Streets.

LCFHS

ST. JAMES CHURCH

This is the St. James Church of the future occupying a square block from Third to Fourth Street and from Market to Dock Street. At the corner of Dock and Fourth Street in the foreground is the building that will replace the Fire Department Headquarters.

FIRST PRESBYTERIAN CHURCH

LCFHS

Located at South Front Street, the above church only lasted from 1818 until a fire in 1819.

NHCPL

On the east side of South Front Street between Dock and Orange Streets, the above church was used from 1820 until a fire destroyed it in 1859.

NHCPL

The above church was built on the northeast corner of Third and Orange Streets in 1861. Woodrow Wilson's father, Joseph, was pastor from 1874 - 1885. A fire on December 31, 1925 ruined it.

LCFHS

At the same location as its predecessor, the above church has been in use since 1928.

CHURCHES

ST. THOMAS CATHOLIC CHURCH

LCFHS

The above church was completed in 1847 at 208 Dock Street. It was in use as a church until it was damaged in a 1968 fire. Afterward its parishioners went to St. Mary Catholic Church, and it has since been used for the performing arts.

ST. MARY CATHOLIC CHURCH

NHCPL

Located on the northwest corner of Fifth Avenue and Ann Street, St. Mary was dedicated in 1912. It was expected to be the cathedral for the future Diocese of North Carolina, but when the diocese was created in 1924, a smaller church in Raleigh was designated as the cathedral.

FRONT STREET / GRACE METHODIST CHURCH

FRONT STREET METHODIST CHURCH

GRACE METHODIST CHURCH

GRACE METHODIST CHURCH

NHCPL

The above church was built in 1844 at the northeast corner of Front and Walnut Streets. After a fire destroyed it in 1886, the congregation decided to build a church on Mulberry Street.

Completed in 1887 at the northeast corner of Fourth and Mulberry Streets, the church created a street name change. People began to say they were going to Grace Street because of the name of this church. In about 1895 the city officially renamed Mulberry Street. A fire destroyed this church in 1947.

LCFHS

This church has been in use since about 1950.

CHURCHES
ST. STEPHEN A.M.E. CHURCH

ST. STEPHEN

Located at 501 Red Cross Street, Saint Stephen was completed in 1888 after many years of very difficult work by former slaves. It continues in use today.

ST. STEPHEN

The annex was completed in 1914. It includes a school and gymnasium as well as a library and swimming pool.

SOUTHSIDE BAPTIST CHURCH

South Side Baptist Church, Wilmington, N. C.—37

Completed in 1914 at the northwest corner of Fifth Avenue and Wooster Streets, the above church remained in use until 1972. At that time the congregation relocated to the below church at 3320 South College Road.

CHURCHES
ST. JOHN'S EPISCOPAL CHURCH

ST. JOHN'S

The above building was completed in 1853 at the southeast corner of Red Cross and Third Streets. Since 1955 the church has been located (below) at 1219 Forest Hills Drive.

ST. JOHN'S

CHURCHES
ST. NICHOLAS GREEK ORTHODOX CHURCH

PISTOLIS

The first Greek Orthodox Church in the city (above) was built at the southwest corner of Orange and South Front Streets in 1945. After the congregation relocated to South College Road (below) in 1980, the original church became part of St. John's Museum of Art.

KOEPPEL

CHAPTER 18

SCHOOLS
TILESTON

NHCPL

Located on the south side of Ann Street between Fourth Street and Fifth Avenue, the above school was completed in 1872 and provided elementary education until 1900. At that time, it became known as Wilmington High School and served in that capacity until 1921 when New Hanover High School was completed on Market Street. The expansion of the size of the school is shown below.

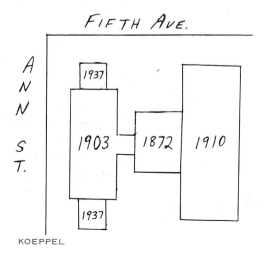

KOEPPEL

NHCPL

Wilmington High School appears above in 1905. After 1920 it became Tileston Elementary until 1970. It was then closed. St. Mary Church acquired the building in 1989, and has been using it as a school as shown below.

LOWMAN

SCHOOLS
WILLISTON

NHCPL

The Williston Industrial School shown above was built in 1915 for black students. Located on the east side of South Tenth Street between Nun and Church Streets, it was replaced by Williston High School (below) in 1937.

NHCPL

LOWMAN

After 1968 the Williston Middle School (above) came into existence and continues to be used in that capacity.

NHCPL

The first school named Hemenway was built in 1872 on Fourth Street between Red Cross and Campbell Streets. It was replaced in 1889 with a building on Fifth Avenue between Chestnut and Grace Streets. After a fire it was rebuilt in 1897. That school is shown above prior to a second fire. The next school (below) was built in 1915.

NHCPL

LOWMAN

The above park was created after a third fire destroyed a school named Hemenway in 1971. The fence and stone posts at the school entrance are all that remain today.

SCHOOLS

UNION

NHCPL

The above school was at the northeast corner of Sixth and Ann Streets from 1886 - 1923. A prior school with this name was at Sixth Street between Nun and Church Streets. It was built in 1867. As indicated below the appearance of this corner has changed considerably.

LOWMAN

DELGADO / WASHINGTON CATLETT

NHCPL

The first Delgado School (above) was built for the children of employees of Delgado Mills. Located at 2002 Colwell Avenue a more modern facility (below) replaced it in 1914 and was in use until 1978. It was named for the Cape Fear Academy educator.

NHCPL

LOWMAN

It is now being refurbished (above) and will soon be restored to its former appearance.

SCHOOLS

PEABODY

NHCPL

There were a series of schools for black students with this name beginning in 1868. The above facility at 507 North Sixth Street was in use from 1924 - 1984. The below building is serving students at this time.

LOWMAN

NHCPL

Located on Meares Street between Fourth Street and Fifth Avenue, the above school was in use from 1914 - 1984. As shown below it has been converted into apartments.

LOWMAN

SCHOOLS

HARNETT / DUDLEY

NHCPL

The above building at 920 North Sixth Street was in use from 1914 - 1983. In 1952 the name change occurred. A church has acquired the below property and is trying to raise funds to restore it as a learning center.

LOWMAN

Wilmington Then and Now

NHCPL

In 1924 the above school at 2716 Castle Hayne Road was built. It continues to serve students. As shown below a second floor has been added.

LOWMAN

SCHOOLS
NEW HANOVER HIGH SCHOOL

New Hanover High School, Wilmington, N. C.

LCFHS

The above school has been at 1307 Market Street since 1921. It is still in use today and is shown below with Brogden Hall that was added in 1957.

LOWMAN

NHCPL

The above building was built as the Isaac Bear School on the south side of Market Street between 12th and 13th Streets in about 1912. It became the first home to Wilmington College, the prior name of the university, in 1947. After the college relocated to College Road in 1961, it had the appearance shown below. College Road, formerly known as 46th Street, extends through the pines as a two lane road to Market Street.

NHCPL

SCHOOLS
UNIVERSITY OF NORTH CAROLINA AT WILMINGTON

LOWMAN

The university has grown and College Road has expanded.

CHAPTER 19
FIRE DEPARTMENT

NHCPL

The building (above) was designated as the first headquarters in 1875. It was at the corner of Fourth and Princess Streets. The below location at Fourth and Dock Streets shown about 100 years ago has been headquarters for almost the entire history of the department.

NHCPL

FIRE DEPARTMENT

In 1901 a brick headquarters was built at the northwest corner of Fourth and Dock Streets. Horse drawn equipment was still being used above, but trucks had replaced them below, in the 1920's.

In 1956 the above headquarters was opened at Fourth and Dock Streets. In 2000 it was replaced by the new building on Market Street.

Wilmington Then and Now

NHCPL

Fire Engine Company #2 was located on the southwest corner of Fifth Avenue and Castle Street from 1915 - 1956. The building retains its original appearance today in the Dry Pond neighborhood.

LOWMAN

FIRE DEPARTMENT

LOWMAN

Today's Fire Station #2 is shown above at Empie Park. It has been in use since 1966.
Fire Station #3 below on Princess Place Drive was opened in 1973.

LOWMAN

NHCPL

The Brooklyn section of the city was protected by Fire Station #4 from 1907 - 1973. Above horse drawn equipment is shown and below it serves as a fitness center. It is located just south of the railroad bridge on Fourth Street at the northeast corner of Campbell Street.

LOWMAN

LOWMAN

Today's Fire Station #4 is on Wallace Avenue near the Municipal Golf Course. It was opened in 1985.

FIRE DEPARTMENT

LOWMAN

Fire Station #5 (above) was located at the southeast corner of 17th Street and Wrightsville Avenue from 1931 - 1966. Wellington Avenue near New Hanover Hospital has been the home of #5 (below) since 1974.

LOWMAN

FIRE DEPARTMENT

LOWMAN

The first Fire Station #6 is shown (above) on the corner of Willard and Third Streets near Greenfield Lake. After serving from 1942 - 1976, it became the administrative office for the Parks and Recreation Department. The current #6 (below) has been at 3929 Carolina Beach Road since 1985.

LOWMAN

FIRE DEPARTMENT

LOWMAN

Fire Station #7 at the northwest corner of South College Road and Pine Valley Drive was completed in 1999. Fire Stations #8 and #9 are scheduled to be built at the corner of Eastwood Road and Cardinal Drive as well as the corner of Military Cut-Off and Eastwood Road. These buildings will be mirror images of each other. A rendering of one of these buildings is shown below.

SMITH - GAGE ARCHITECTS

FIRE DEPARTMENT

PEREZ

SYNTHESIS

The new headquarters (above) extends from Eighth to Ninth Streets on the north side of Market Street. It was occupied in 2000. The Seagate Fire Station at 6102 Oleander Drive has had volunteers since 1956. Wilmington fire equipment and personnel have been placed at the below location since the 1999 annexation occurred. The city may take full control of this facility in the future.

LOWMAN

FIRE DEPARTMENT
CHANGES IN LOCATIONS OF FIRE DEPARTMENT
BUILDINGS BY THE NUMBERS

1

Howard Relief Co. #1
14 South 4th Street
(1867)

Transferred to headquarters
(1902)

Fire Engine Co. #1
3rd & Chestnut Street
(1867 - 1884)

Hook & Ladder Co. #1
313 Dock Street (1867)

1885 - Became Headquarters when new
wooden building completed

1901 - Brick building built

1956 - New brick building finished.
Operations at 2nd and Market
during construction

2000 - New headquarters at
Market and 8th Streets

2

Fire King Co. #2
Front & Nun Streets
(1867 - 1885)

Little Columbia Fire Co. #2
413 Nun Street (1885 - 1897)

1897 - Transferred to headquarters
1915 - 1956 - 5th and Castle Streets
1956 - 1966 - Operated from headquarters
1966 - Located at Empie Park

3

Vigilant Fire Co. #3
2nd St. between Market & Dock Streets
(1867 - 1885)

Cape Fear Steam Fire Engine Co. #3
110 Ann Street (1885 - 1897)

1897 - Transferred to headquarters

1907 - 1965 - Fireboat Station
Fireboat operations handled by
headquarters (1965 - 1984) Fireboat
operations handled by Carolina
Beach Road Fire House since 1984

1973 - Princess Place Drive opened

4

Brooklyn Fire Engine Co. #4
4th Street between Bladen
and Brunswick Streets
(1867 - 1875)

1875 - Little Giant Steam Fire Engine #4
322 Princess Street, first headquarters

1885 - Transferred to new headquarters
at 313 Dock Street

1907 - 4th and Campbell Streets opened

1973 - Operations transferred to
Princess Place Drive #3

1985 - Wallace Avenue - Municipal Golf
Course location opened

5

1931 - 17th and Wrightsville opened

1966 - Operations transferred
to headquarters

1974 - Wellington Avenue opened

FIRE DEPARTMENT
CHANGES IN LOCATIONS OF FIRE DEPARTMENT
BUILDINGS BY THE NUMBERS (CONTINUED)

6

1942 - 3rd and Willard Streets opened

1976 - Operations transferred
to headquarters

1985 - Carolina Beach Road opened

7

1999 - Pine Valley and South
College Road opened

8

2000 - Eastwood Road and
Cardinal Drive to open

9

2000 - Military Cut-Off and
Eastwood Road to open

1999 - City Fire Department equipment placed at
Seagate Volunteer Station at 6102 Oleander Drive
following phase one annexation. Perhaps this will
be designated as #10 in the future.

CHAPTER 20

HOTELS & THEATERS
HOTEL WILMINGTON

NHCPL

Located at the southeast corner of North Front and Walnut Streets from 1914 - 1974, this was one of the city's most prestigious hotels until a few years before it was demolished. Today an empty lot (below) awaits development.

LOWMAN

LCFHS

This hotel was built in 1923 at the northwest corner of Second and Chestnut Streets. In recent years it has been converted to apartments.

LCFHS   NHCPL

The similarity between 1930 (left) and the 1990's (right) shows the passage of years does not always bring great changes.

HOTELS & THEATERS
ORTON HOTEL / ROYAL THEATER

NHCPL

The Orton Hotel (above) was built at 115 North Front Street in 1886. Until the 1920's it was probably the city's best hotel. In 1915 The Royal Theater (below at left) was built slightly to the north. Both were destroyed in a disastrous fire in 1949.

LCFHS

LOWMAN

This portion of North Front Street (above right) shows the new buildings constructed after the fire.

CAPE FEAR MUSEUM

The Cowan House (above) was on the west side of North Front Street between Chestnut and Grace Streets. It was demolished in 1906 and the Bijou Theater (below left) was built to replace it. The beauty of the front facade could not prevent the theater from closing in 1956 or being torn down in 1963

NHCPL

LOWMAN

Today all that remains is the mosaic of the name (above right). A park has been created where the theater once stood.

HOTELS & THEATERS
BROOKLYN THEATER

NHCPL

This theater was on the east side of North Fourth Street between Brunswick and Bladen Streets. It was built around 1910 and was closed before the end of the 1950's. The building below has survived and is used for private purposes.

LOWMAN

HOTELS & THEATERS
BONITZ HOTEL
VICTORIA - CAROLINA - COLONY THEATER

NHCPL

The Bonitz Hotel (above) was built in 1890 at 120 Market Street. It was replaced by the Victoria Theater (below left) in 1912. The name was changed to Carolina in 1934 when sound equipment was installed. In 1953 it became the Colony Theater.

LCFHS

LOWMAN

The Colony closed in 1974 and was demolished in 1976. Today (above right) the corner of Second and Market Streets is a parking lot. The building on the left is the same building that was to the left of the Bonitz Hotel.

HOTELS & THEATERS
GRAND THEATER

NHCPL

Located at 23-27 North Front Street just north of the Masonic building, the Grand Theater (above) operated from 1913 - 1923. After that time it was used for retail purposes. The building (right) still stands beside the Masonic building.

LOWMAN

CREST THEATER

CREASY

The Crest Theater (above) was on the east side of North Lumina Avenue in Wrightsville Beach. It opened in the 1940's and closed in the 1970's. It is shown below in the 1990's.

LOWMAN

MANOR THEATER

CAPE FEAR MUSEUM

The Manor Theater (above) opened at 208 Market Street in 1941 and closed in 1985. Today a club (below) is located in the building.

KOEPPEL

BAILEY THEATER

W-8—Front Street, Looking North, Wilmington, N. C.

LCFHS

The Bailey Theater (above) shown a few years after it opened in 1940 at 18 North Front Street. It was the city's first air-conditioned theater. It closed in 1980. The facade (below) is all that remains today.

KOEPPEL

CHAPTER 21
WINTER PARK

RIVENBARK

Looking north in the early 1950's, Oleander Drive is the road proceeding east and west closest to the foreground. College Road, then called 46th Street, is at the lower left and went north only as far as Wrightsville Avenue. It would not be extended to Market Street and beyond until plans were made to relocate Wilmington College to the existing UNCW area. Pine Grove Road extends diagonally to the southeast from Wrightsville Avenue left of center. Kerr Avenue heads north from this location.

RIVENBARK

Looking west in the 1950's, College Road has two lanes extending from the lower left corner. Oleander Drive proceeds from the right foreground and bends to the west left of center. Just beyond the bend and to the left is Carl Dunn's Airport for private planes. This is east of the 1990's Independence Mall. On the north side of Oleander slightly west of the airport is a drive-in theater. It is on the west side of Floral Parkway. The Winter Park Presbyterian Church is to the right of the intersection of Pine Grove Avenue and Wrightsville Avenue at the middle right.

WINTER PARK

LOWMAN

Looking north in the 1990's College Road extends from top to bottom in the center. Oleander Drive crosses the middle. A relatively small crossroads of the 1950's has become a major intersection. The trees at the lower right are part of Hugh MacRae Park.

CHAPTER 22
MERCHANTS
DELGADO / SPOFFORD MILLS

LCFHS

The largest employer in the area during the first half of the 20th century other than the railroad, Delgado Mills (above) was established in 1899. Located on the north side of Wrightsville Avenue west of Burnt Mill Creek, the important dates in its existence as well as a rear view are below.

> 1933 - name changed to Spofford Mills
> 1967 - closed due to foreign competition
> 1971 - buildings demolished

NHCPL

KOEPPEL

In the 1970's the Creek Apartments (above) were built at this location.

MERCHANTS
TIDE WATER POWER CO. / CAROLINA POWER & LIGHT

CP&L

Located at the southwest corner of Fourth and Chestnut Streets the building (above) was built in 1950. After Carolina Power & Light bought Tide Water Power in 1952, they occupied it until New Hanover County acquired it in the 1970's. Local headquarters of CP&L are now at the southeast corner of Eastwood Road and Military Cut-off. (below)

LOWMAN

NHCPL

The power for Tide Water Power Company was generated (above) at a plant where Castle Street meets the Cape Fear River. This is the current location of Solomon Towers since 1970. The L. V. Sutton Plant (below) was built by Carolina Power & Light in 1954 northwest of the city. It is named for a former CP&L chief executive officer.

CP&L

MERCHANTS
SOUTHERN BELL / BELL SOUTH

LOWMAN

Although originally at the northwest corner of Front and Princess Streets, in 1903 Southern Bell Telephone & Telegraph occupied 125 Princess Street (above) at the northwest corner of Second Street. A new headquarters (below) was built in 1936 at the northeast corner of Fourth and Princess Streets.

LOWMAN

LOWMAN

Southern Bell's need to expand resulted in an adjacent location in 1967 (above) at the northwest corner of Fifth Avenue and Princess Street. As indicated, the company is now Bell South.

LOWMAN

Although the entrance (above) at the southwest corner of Orange and South Front Streets was built in the 1950's, this company can trace its origins to 1838. The operations extended to Water Street. In 1999 the oldest company in the city relocated (below) to the west side of 13th Street between Meares and Marstellar Streets.

LOWMAN

MERCHANTS
HANOVER IRON WORKS

As indicated (above) this company was located at 111 Water Street after being established in 1903. By the 1960's prosperity and the need for a larger facility resulted in a relocation (below) to 1851 Dawson Street.

HANOVER IRON WORKS

CAPE FEAR MUSEUM

Although MacMillan & Cameron opened a service station at the southwest corner of Third and Chestnut Streets in 1923, they replaced it with the building above in 1939. The night view (below) does not diminish the quality of the structure.

CAMERON

LOWMAN

After the service station closed in 1962, United Carolina Bank (now BB&T) opened a regional headquarters (above) in 1987.

MERCHANTS
HUGHES BROTHERS

HUGHES BROTHERS

In the 1920's (above) at the northeast corner of Second and Market Streets, Hughes Brothers began to service automobiles. Cooperative Bank is now at that location. By the early 1930's the company moved to 1101 Market Street (below).

HUGHES BROTHERS

HUGHES BROTHERS

NHCPL

The current building (above) was completed at 1110 Market Street in 1935. By the 1950's (below) a new set of letters was being used for the company name and the gasoline pumps were modernized.

HUGHES BROTHERS

LOWMAN

Although the house to the east on the right was demolished and gasoline pumps were removed, the 1990's (above) are very similar to the 1950's.

MERCHANTS
GAYLORD'S / BELK - WILLIAMS

NHCPL

At what would today be 226 North Front Street (above) a department store was opened by Brady & Gaylord in 1888. The dates below are significant.

1897 - The store becomes known as Gaylord's.

1916 - Belk - Williams (right) buys Gaylord's and occupies the location until 1951

BELK - BEERY

BELK - BEERY

CAPE FEAR MUSEUM

At the northeast corner of Second and Chestnut Streets (above) Dr. Wood practiced medicine. Belk - Williams bought the property, built a store in 1951 (below) and named it Belk - Beery. This building has been the New Hanover Public Library since the 1980's.

BELK - BEERY

LOWMAN

Belk - Beery moved to Independence Mall (above) in 1979 when the mall opened. At that time the store at Second and Chestnut was vacated, and it later became a library.

MERCHANTS
EINSTEIN BROTHERS / EFIRD'S

NHCPL

The building above, at the southeast corner of Grace and North Front Streets, was occupied by Einstein Brothers Department Store until 1921. From that time until the early 1970's it was home to Efird's Department Store. Although the upper floors are now occupied (right), the ground floor is vacant.

LOWMAN

ANDREWS MORTUARY

ANDREWS MORTUARY

Although this company has been serving the people of the city since 1850, the building at 419 North Third Street at Red Cross Street (above) was not occupied until 1934. After purchasing the home (below) at 1617 Market Street, it was renovated and has been open for business since 1961.

ANDREWS MORTUARY

MERCHANTS
RHODES FURNITURE

RHODES FURNITURE

After having been a prominent company in the South for many years, Rhodes arrived in the city in the 1950's (above) at 310 North Front Street. This location was occupied by the store until it was relocated at 460 South College Road (below) in 1974.

KOEPPEL

MERCHANTS
SUTTON - COUNCIL FURNITURE

SUTTON

This business was established in 1924 and occupied the building at 313 North Front Street (above) from 1951 to 1974. This location is now part of the Cotton Exchange. The store on South College Road (below) provided furniture to its customers from 1974 - 1999.

SUTTON

MERCHANTS
COASTAL MOTORS / RIPPY AUTO PARK

RIPPY

Beginning in 1946 at the southwest corner of Eleventh and Market Streets (above), Coastal Motors sold Cadillacs and Oldsmobiles. In 1970 the name was changed after J. Fred Rippy, Jr. became the sole owner. In 1990 the company began selling Mitsubishis. A new showroom (below) was opened at 4951 New Centre Drive in 1995.

KOEPPEL

D&E

After Marion DuBose entered business as a used car dealer in 1947 at Third and Martin Streets, he gradually expanded the company. After acquiring the Dodge and Jeep franchises in 1965 and 1968 respectively, he relocated to 6220 Market Street (above) in 1971. With the guidance of Jeff DuBose, the Jeep Eagle operations were placed in the acquired building (below) at the right.

D&E

MERCHANTS
CAPE FEAR FORD

CAPE FEAR FORD

This company began selling Fords on the north side of Market Street between Second and Third Streets (above) in the 1930's. The location is shown in 1959. Bill and P.C. Smith relocated operations to 4222 Oleander Drive (below) in 1967.

LOWMAN

RANEY

After acquiring the Chevrolet franchise in the 1920's, the Raneys expanded their operations at the southeast corner of Fourth and Princess Streets (above) in the early 1950's. The Sheriff's Department building is currently at this location. Under the leadership of Bill Raney the company moved to 228 South College Road (below) in 1971. After a series of ownership changes, it is now Jeff Gordon Chevrolet.

JEFF GORDON

MERCHANTS
COOPERATIVE BANK

COOPERATIVE

The oldest bank that has its roots in the city, Cooperative Bank began operations at 124 Princess Street (above) in 1898. Frederick Willetts, Sr., with the assistance of his son Frederick Willetts, Jr., moved the bank to 8 North Front Street (below) in 1949.

COOPERATIVE

COOPERATIVE

At the northeast corner of Second and Market Streets (above) Cooperative opened a new headquarters in 1959. Rick Willetts is guiding the bank into the 21st Century.

REEDS JEWELERS

REEDS

This business was established by Bill and Roberta Zimmer at 7 North Front Street (above) in 1946. During the 1960's, the store moved to 27 North Front Street (below). Alan Zimmer has expanded operations to include about 100 locations.

LOWMAN

MERCHANTS
KINGOFF'S JEWELERS

KINGOFF

KINGOFF

There has not always been a clock in front of this store. The original location at 300 North Front Street (above) in the 1920's is at the northeast corner of Grace Street. Since 1937 business has been conducted at 10-12 North Front Street (left).

A change in the front of the store (right) as well as the clock shows how the location appears today.

KINGOFF

Viewed from Water Street (above) in 1973, this area required the expertise of talented people to avoid demolition. Fortunately, Mal Murray and Joe Reeves were living in the city. They revitalized the warehouses and industrial buildings by transforming them (below) into stores and creating a place where tourists and residents can shop.

Wilmington Then and Now

MERCHANTS
J.H. REHDER & CO.

NHCPL

Located at 617 North Fourth Street (above) since the 1880's, this company anchored a significant retail district that existed in the Brooklyn neighborhood. During the 1930's the business became a victim of the Depression. It was on the west side of Fourth Street north of the railroad bridge (below). Today an empty lot awaits development. J.H. Rehder was part of the family currently known for their floral abilities.

LOWMAN

Castle Street has been a retail area for many years. M.G. Tiencken owned the store (above) at the southeast corner of South Fourth and Castle Streets as shown about 1900. It was later sold to William Beery who became associated with Belk department stores. Now this location is no longer used for commercial purposes.

CHAPTER 23

BUILDINGS

NHCPL   NHCPL

The City Market (above left) is the building that gave Market Street its name. It was located near the intersection of Market and Water Streets until 1881. The replacement building was constructed on the west side of South Front Street between Dock and Orange Streets (above right) and retained the facade with the two steeples until the late 1920's.

LOWMAN

The existing building (above) has the original walls but without the sign at the front, it may not be recognized as a structure from the 1880's.

NHCPL

The Custom House (above) was built in 1843 on the east side of Water Street between Market and Princess Streets. It was demolished in 1915 to enable the existing Federal Building (below) to be built. The ferry boat transported people and vehicles across the river from the foot of Market Street until the late 1920's when the bridges north of the city were completed. To the left of the Federal Building is the Maffitt Building. The Murchison Building is at the far left, and the Trust Building is on the right.

NHCPL

BUILDINGS

The northeast corner of Front and Market Streets (at left) was the location of William H. Green Company until the Trust Building (below) became the city's tallest building upon completion in 1912.

Wilmington Then and Now

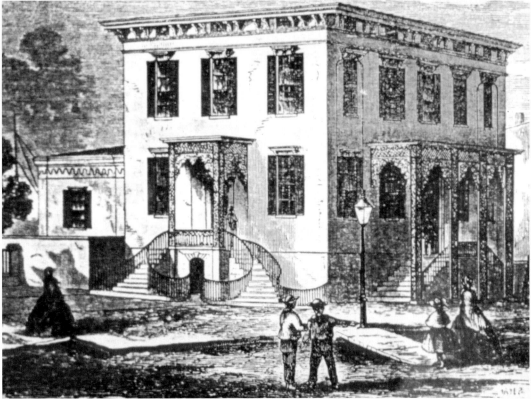

NHCPL

Located on the west side of Front Street between Market and Princess Streets (above) the Cape Fear Bank had originally been built as a home for John Ancrum, an eighteenth century merchant. It was demolished in 1899 when the Masonic Building (below) was built.

NHCPL

BUILDINGS

DARE

The southwest corner of Front and Princess Streets (above) was the location of a bank building in about 1980 that looked as if it had been recently built. As a result of an excellent restoration project, the building (right) has been restored to its original appearance and is now the Paleo Sun Cafe.

LOWMAN

NHCPL

The northwest corner of Front and Princess Streets (above) had been a location for banks since 1873 when the Bank of New Hanover became the first one to occupy this building. Later known as The People's Savings Bank, this structure was demolished in 1959 when Wachovia Bank (below) constructed the present building.

LOWMAN

BUILDINGS

CAPE FEAR MUSEUM

Built in 1904 at the southwest corner of Front and Chestnut Streets (above) the Southern Building remained at this location until 1959. The Bank of America (below) now occupies this corner.

LOWMAN

N.C. DIV. OF ARCH. & HIST.

The Dickinson House (above) was built at the northeast corner of Front and Chestnut Streets in 1851. It remained at this location until it was demolished to build the Acme Building (below) that was completed in 1902. The Murchison National Bank was here from that time until it moved across the street about fifteen years later. Home Savings Bank and Morris Plan Bank also occupied this building. Today it is a private residence.

NHCPL

BUILDINGS

NHCPL

In 1913 the Wilmington Savings and Trust Co. (above) was located on the south side of Princess Street between Front and Second Streets. The bank was later acquired by Wachovia Bank. The building was demolished in the early 1960's and a parking lot (below) is now present at this site.

LOWMAN

NHCPL

The Acme Saloon (above) was at the northeast corner of Front and Dock Streets until it was forced to close in 1910 due to state prohibition. Shortly thereafter Roudabush's Seed Co. (below) began its business at this location.

KOEPPEL

BUILDINGS

LCFHS

When George Washington visited the city, he slept in the building (above) at the southeast corner of Dock and Front Streets. A granite marker (below) to the right of the fire hydrant in the foreground makes note of this fact. The building was demolished in 1921, and a parking lot now occupies this location. The steeple of the First Presbyterian Church is at the upper left.

KOEPPEL

N.C. DIV. OF ARCH. & HIST.

The northwest corner of Third and Market Streets (above) was the location of the Armand DeRosset House. It was built before 1800 and served as the Confederate Army Headquarters. A service station (below) replaced it in 1919.

WELLS

LOWMAN

After extensive renovations Harold W. Wells & Son (above) occupied this building in about 1970.

BUILDINGS

St. John's Tavern,
Wilmington, N. C.

LCFHS

On the south side of Orange Street between Second and Front Streets (above) St. John's Tavern was built in 1804 as St. John's Lodge, the oldest Masonic Lodge in North Carolina. It became the home of St. John's Museum of Art in 1962. After the year 2000, it will be moving to the southeast corner of 17th Street and Independence Boulevard (below) and will be renamed the Louise Wells Cameron Art Museum as a result of the generosity of the Cameron family.

ST. JOHN'S MUSEUM OF ART

CHAPTER 24

HOMES

NHCPL

Located at 400 South Front Street, the house (above) was built in 1825 for Edward Dudley, the first popularly elected governor of North Carolina. After James Sprunt purchased it in the 1890's, he had a second floor added to the wings on each side (below) as well as four columns at the front to support the high portico.

NHCPL

LCFHS

After the Sprunt family sold the house in the 1920's, the columns and portico were removed (above). The appearance has not changed significantly since then.

HOMES

NHCPL

After 1900 Pembroke Jones bought a large tract of land north of today's Eastwood Road overlooking the Intracoastal Waterway. He built a hunting lodge (above) that he used until 1919. After a fire in the 1950's, the property was transferred to the company that renamed the area Landfall (below) in the 1980's. It is still being developed as a community of private homes.

LANDFALL

LCFHS

Located at the southwest corner of Dock and South Third Streets (above), the Bridgers House was completed in 1906. St. Thomas Church is at the right. After remaining a private residence until 1944, the building (below) became the American Legion Home.

Wilmington Post No. 10,
American Legion Home,
Wilmington, N. C.

LCFHS

GRAYSTONE

The American Legion remained until 1972. After being used for a variety of purposes, the building was restored to its original elegance and is now the Graystone Inn (above)

CHAPTER 25

CLUBS & ORGANIZATIONS
CAPE FEAR CLUB

NHCPL   NHCPL

The James Dawson House (above left) was occupied by the Cape Fear Club 1888 - 1913. It was located at 201 North Front Street where the First Union Bank Building (above right) stands today. The clubhouse at 206 Chestnut Street (below) was opened on November 14, 1913.

LOWMAN

CLUBS & ORGANIZATIONS
BRIGADE BOYS & GIRLS CLUB

NHCPL

The Armory (above) at the southeast corner of Second and Church Streets was dedicated on June 23, 1905. It remained in use until 1950.

BRIGADE CLUB

A new clubhouse (above) was occupied in 1950 at 718 South Third Street. Due to heavy traffic, it was vacated in 1987, and activities have been at 2759 Vance Street (below) since then.

LOWMAN

CLUBS & ORGANIZATIONS
CAPE FEAR COUNTRY CLUB

NHCPL

The original clubhouse (above) was built in the 1890's shortly after the club was established in 1896. Today's facility (below) was built in 1922.

NHCPL

CLUBS & ORGANIZATIONS
YMCA

NHCPL

The above building at the northwest corner of Grace and North Front Streets housed the YMCA after it was built in 1891. After the YMCA left in 1913, it became a hotel. Known first as the Imperial, it later was called the Carolina, and the Brunswick Hotel before becoming a furniture store in the 1950's and being demolished in 1970. It is now a parking lot as is the building below.

NHCPL

The north side of Market Street between Third and Fourth Streets was the YMCA home from 1913 - 1968. The George Davis monument and half of the Colonial Apartments are on the left, and Dr. John Cranmer's house is at the right.

LOWMAN

Since the 1960's the YMCA has been at 2710 Market Street.

CLUBS & ORGANIZATIONS
YWCA

NHCPL

The YWCA was located at 708 Market Street (above) from 1948 - 1974. It has been at 2815 South College Road (below) since then.

LOWMAN

CHAPTER 26
AIR & SEA PORTS
AIRPORT

WIA

The airport (above) was named Wilmington in 1927 before being renamed for World War I hero Arthur Bluethenthal the next year. Its runways (below) are north of Smith Creek, the wavy line in the foreground. The thin line above the upper runway and parallel to it is Gordon Road when it extended from North Kerr Ave. to Castle Hayne Road.

WIA

AIR & SEA PORTS
AIRPORT

TOM & JERRY

The airport opened the passenger terminal (above) in 1951. It served the area until it was replaced in 1990 by the existing terminal (below). It is now known as Wilmington International Airport.

WIA

SEAPORT

NHCPL

The seaport (above) was located south of Sunset Park in the early 1940's. Its purpose was to build liberty ships (below) during World War II. The road to this area is still called Shipyard Boulevard.

STATE PORT

AIR & SEA PORTS
SEAPORT

STATE PORT

After World War II, the State Port Authority was created to promote ocean trade. Its modest beginnings (above) have expanded into a modern facility (below) attracting commerce throughout the world.

STATE PORT

CHAPTER 27

HOSPITALS
MARINE HOSPITAL

NHCPL

Built by James Walker in 1857 at the southeast corner of Eighth and Nun Streets, the above hospital was closed in 1900. It housed German prisoners during both World Wars. From 1923 - 1942 it was used by the North Carolina National Guard. The city used it for storage from 1945 - 1958, and then it was demolished.

CITY HOSPITAL

NHCPL

Organized in 1881 and located at Tenth and Red Cross Streets the above hospital remained in use until 1901.

HOSPITALS
JAMES WALKER MEMORIAL HOSPITAL

NHCPL

Located on the site of City Hospital, the facility (above) - designed by and named for James Walker - opened in 1901 shortly after Walker died. The northwest wing (below) was completed in 1943.

NHCPL

NHCPL

This aerial view shows the hospital at its greatest extent in about 1963. Tenth Street is in the foreground. The former nurses residence (below) was the only building that was not demolished in 1972. It is now a residence for the elderly.

LOWMAN

HOSPITALS
COMMUNITY HOSPITAL

NHCPL

Located at 415 North Seventh Street the above hospital served black people from 1920-1938. The below hospital was built with Works Progress Administration funds in 1938. It was located on South Eleventh Street. The nurses home is on the left. It retained the same name and was in use until New Hanover Hospital was completed in 1967.

NHCPL

HARPER'S SANITARIUM

This private hospital was at the northeast corner of South Front and Castle Streets. It was operated by Dr. Charles Harper from 1910 - 1916. He was the nephew of John Harper, the captain of the steamer *Wilmington* that was used for excursions. The below view indicates that there is no trace of the sanitarium today.

HOSPITALS
THE BABIES HOSPITAL

NHCPL

Founded by Dr. James Buren Sidbury in 1920 on Wrightsville Avenue at Wrightsville Sound, the above hospital was replaced in 1927 by the hospital below.

NHCPL

NHCPL

The third floor was added to the left and right sides of the hospital in the late 1940's. Dr. Sidbury died in 1967 and the hospital closed in 1978. Today it is used for offices.

Wilmington Then and Now

CAPE FEAR HOSPITAL

NHCPL

This hospital is located at 5301 Wrightsville Avenue. It is shown above shortly after its 1958 opening. Its current appearance, when merged into New Hanover Hospital, is shown below.

NEW HANOVER HOSPITAL

HOSPITALS
NEW HANOVER REGIONAL MEDICAL CENTER

NHCPL

The above hospital at 2131 South 17th Street was completed in 1967 following the efforts of Dr. Robert Fales, among others, to promote the passage of a bond issue. The appearance below indicates growth is still continuing.

NEW HANOVER HOSPITAL

New Hanover Health Network
NEW HANOVER HOSPITAL

The full extent of the hospital and its facilities is indicated above. The recently completed Zimmer Cancer Research Center below is primarily a result of the generosity of the family associated with Reeds Jewelers.

NEW HANOVER HOSPITAL

CREASY

The beach area in 1929 (above) had much less land. At the north end of the island is Moore's Inlet that separated Wrightsville Beach from Shell Island. The inlet did not exist after 1967. By the 1980's (below) all but the north end of Shell Island (center below Mason inlet at top) had been developed.

TOM & JERRY'S

WRIGHTSVILLE BEACH
AERIAL VIEWS

NHCPL

The trolley line (at left center above) can be seen approaching the beach and winding south in 1929. Just north of this area and extending to the ocean is the Oceanic Hotel. Homes did not extend beyond Augusta Street at the north. In the 1970's (below) Waynick Boulevard is in the foreground. It had been built in 1936 with sand from Banks Channel. Newell's store is the former Station #1 to the right of the intersection near the bridge.

CREASY

WRIGHTSVILLE BEACH
HARBOR ISLAND

NHCPL

Originally called Shore Acres, in 1926 (above) a bridge and causeway had just been completed (left center) allowing cars in this area for the first time. The street layout still exists. The Harbor Island Auditorium is at the right center. In the 1990's (below) there are many homes and trees. Seapath Towers is the building at left center. In 1964 Harbor Island was annexed by Wrightsville Beach.

CREASY

WRIGHTSVILLE BEACH
HARBOR ISLAND

The auditorium (above) existed from 1916 - 1930. Although it was a center of social activity, it did not recruit enough functions to continue. In recent years International Nickel, now LaQue Center, built a facility (below) to study corrosion at this location.

WRIGHTSVILLE BEACH
GETTING THERE

NHCPL

Before a steam railroad line was built in the 1880's the beach could only be reached by boat. After 1902 the electric trolley line (above) replaced the train. Harbor Island Auditorium is on the north side of Banks Channel. The footbridge (below) crosses Banks Channel to the beach. The Oceanic Hotel is to the left of the trolley.

NHCPL

NHCPL

Looking east, the causeway (above) opened in 1926 to the south of the trolley line on the left and allowed cars to cross Wrightsville Sound and reach Harbor Island for the first time. Looking east (below) towards the beach, the causeway passes through an undeveloped Harbor Island.

NHCPL

NHCPL

A drawbridge (above) was present in the 1930's to allow boats utilizing the newly completed Intracoastal Waterway to proceed. The Tidewater Power Company building is on the mainland (center). Traffic jams going to Harbor Island (below) delayed cars just as they do today. Babies Hospital is barely visible at the upper right.

NHCPL

LCFHS

The bridge over Banks Channel (above) was completed in 1935. The trolleys were no longer economical and service ended in 1940. A new bridge in 1958 replaced the drawbridge (below) that spanned Wrightsville Sound. Both are shown before the drawbridge was removed.

NHCPL

TOM & JERRY'S

The existing Banks Channel bridge and Station One Condominiums in the right foreground show the area as it appeared in the 1990's (above).

WRIGHTSVILLE BEACH
AT THE BEACH

NHCPL

Station One (above) was located just east of the Banks Channel Bridge. The tracks on the left went south to Station Seven and Lumina. The others went north beyond the Oceanic Hotel. After trolley service ended, Station One was enclosed and became Newell's Store. In 1992 Newell's was bought by Wings (below). The trolley line to Lumina had passed between the two telephone poles to the right of Wings.

LOWMAN

CREASY

At the lower right (above) is Station One in about 1930. Looking south, two parallel boardwalks were on each side of the tracks. It is not difficult to imagine life at the beach (below) before the arrival of cars when observing this view looking north about half-way between Lumina and Station One.

NHCPL

WRIGHTSVILLE BEACH
AT THE BEACH

NHCPL

Looking north (above) at the point where Lumina Avenue meets the approach to the bridge in 1937, cars have become plentiful. At the same location (below) in 1999 it is ironic that cars are almost completely absent.

LOWMAN

LCFHS

In 1905 the Tarrymore Hotel (above) was opened just north of Station One. It extended from Banks Channel to the Ocean. This view is from the channel. The south side of the hotel is below. After the 1911 season it was sold and renamed the Oceanic Hotel.

CREASY

WRIGHTSVILLE BEACH
OCEANIC HOTEL

OCEANIC HOTEL, WRIGHTSVILLE BEACH,
WILMINGTON, N. C.—53

NHCPL

After acquiring this hotel (above) for the 1912 season, the new owners built a three level balcony above the entrance. The fishermen (below) made sure the hotel guests were never hungry. The Oceanic was destroyed in a 1934 fire that affected all of the northern part of the community.

The Fishermen's Dock in front of Oceanic Hotel,
Wrightsville Beach, near Wilmington, N. C.

NHCPL

LCFHS

The fire began on the northern part of the island at Kitty Cottage (above) in January. The strong winter winds helped it to rapidly spread. Carolina Cottage (below) was another of the buildings that was completely destroyed.

CREASY

WRIGHTSVILLE BEACH
SEASHORE HOTEL

The hotel (above) was built in 1897. If all these ocean bathers were sleeping there, they filled it to capacity. Another view (below) shows the hotel shortly before its name changed to the Ocean Terrace in 1937.

CREASY

The long veranda (above) highlights the west side of the hotel that faced Banks Channel. After Hurricane Hazel in 1954, considerable damage was present, and the hotel closed after a 1956 fire. The Blockade Runner (below) was built at this location in 1962.

BLOCKADE RUNNER

WRIGHTSVILLE BEACH
LUMINA

NHCPL

Built in 1905 at Station 7 at the south end of the trolley line, Lumina had a large dance floor and was the social heart of the beach. A movie screen was installed at the edge of the ocean (above, right) and seats were built along the veranda facing the ocean for viewing. A later view (below) shows that the screen has been removed.

NHCPL

NHCPL

The Pomander Cottages (above) were located between Lumina and Banks Channel. In 1964 (below) Lumina was still an impressive location.

LCFHS

NHCPL

A fishing pier (above) had been built by 1969. It is on the ocean side of the Oceanic Restaurant (below). To the left are the apartments that were built after Lumina was demolished in 1973. The loss of Lumina is arguably the greatest architectural loss in the history of the beach.

LOWMAN

ABOUT THE AUTHOR

Andy Koeppel was the president of an appliance manufacturing company in the Northeast before relocating to Wilmington. Although he always had an interest in history, Andy finds that local history since 1900 is particularly meaningful.

When we look at the streets of America between 1900 and 1940, we can have a much better understanding of the type of life our parents and grandparents experienced when they were children and young adults. What they witnessed influenced their values and our culture. Their thoughts instilled the present generations with many of the ideas that are still evolving in today's world.

This book is the result of Andy's desire to learn more about how Wilmington evolved into the city that he is proud to call his home. He lives near the Pine Valley subdivision with his wife Eileen, with whom he has a daughter and two sons.

INDEX

ML

11/04